ENCOUNTERING MARX

Bonds and Barriers between Christians and Marxists

ENCOUNTERING MARX

Bonds and Barriers between Christians and Marxists

JAN MILIC LOCHMAN

Translated from the German by
Edwin Robertson

CHRISTIAN JOURNALS LIMITED
BELFAST

First English Edition 1977 by Christian Journals Limited, Belfast

Originally published in German as *Marx begegnen* © 1975. by Gütersloher Verlagshaus Gerd Mohn.

Copyright © Christian Journals Limited 1977.

Cover by Joe Hynes and Trevor Andrews

ISBN 0 904302 23 7

Made and printed in Ireland

Contents

Translator's Note

The importance of this book lies in its origin in Czechoslovakia, 1968. For a brief period, Christian theologians and Marxist philosophers met and the excitement of the encounter almost gave to Communism a human face. What it did for Christianity was equally important. Jan Milič Lochman, a systematic theologian now at the University of Basel in Switzerland, came out of the heart of that encounter. In this book he introduces us to the writings of the young Karl Marx, papers only recently published, whose impact has not yet been felt by Christians as it should be and whose importance was recognized by doctrinaire Marxists and suppressed. The tanks that rolled into Prague in 1968 were to protect the people of Czechoslovakia, not from the declining powers of the West, but from the young Karl Marx. Jan Lochman also introduces us to Ernst Bloch, whose writings have scarcely spread outside his native Germany. A whole area of discussion, dialogue, encounter was opened between Marxists and Christians. Jan Milič Lochman has written this book in order that the dialogue may continue. Time will tell whether this dialogue or the Russian tank is more powerful. This book should help to tip the balance in favour of dialogue.

Edwin Robertson

Preface

This book is a plea for an encounter in dialogue with
Marxist thought. It arises out of the author's own
encounters with his Marxist colleagues in Czechoslovakia and later in other European countries.
Particularly since the shattering of the European
dialogue in 1968 and the need to strike a proper balance
in our conversations with Marxists, it has been my
dearest concern to find the right theological orientation
for today.

The book bears marks of its origin. That is at once
obvious in the choice of subject. So long as dialogue
continues with the Marxists of a Socialist country, the
Christian theologian must raise questions about the
meaning of the Biblical heritage in an officially atheist
society. Of all the writings of Karl Marx those that are
most important for this discussion are those of the
young Marx. The study of these will be of value not
only to Marxists who have neglected this part of his
writings, to their great loss, but to all citizens of a
Socialist state—Christians and Marxists—because of
the special attention given in them to the question of
personal alienation and the ways in which it can be
overcome.

There are other themes and writings which should be considered in the context of the discussion between Marxists and Christians, questions concerned with the structure of society, or the theory of class struggle. These will also be dealt with. Meanwhile, I hope that the questions I have faced will be recognized as central for Christians, Marxists and others aware of the problems of our time. They were posed in the East, but are also relevant in the West, they are therefore our problems. My experience in many church groups, in further discussion with Marxists—especially the wise and radical Swiss, my friend, Konrad Farner—encourages me to believe that this book about encounters with Marxists will be welcomed.

Basel.   Jan Milič Lochman

Introduction

Theological Considerations of Marxist Theory

During my first few years as an East European theologian teaching in the West my strongest impression was that of the vital interest of young theologians in Marxist theory. I was not prepared for this. It was so unlike my two decades of teaching in Prague. Of course, we were all aware of Marxist thinking and many of us were busily concerned with understanding it. Marxism-Leninism was the official ideology of our world. Without seriously studying this ideology we could scarcely survive as theologians in a socialist state— both on theological and on political grounds. And then there was always my old teacher, Josef L. Hromadka, constantly urging us to 'take Marxism seriously'.

I fully approved of this advice of Hromadka for my academic and my theological work and tried to follow it. For this reason, I held seminars and lectures regularly with the students of the Comenius Faculty on this subject. We included occasional guests from other faculties. We concentrated upon those texts which were often neglected in the official Marxist teaching, particularly the writings of the young Karl Marx.

Students generally, however, were not inclined to

show much interest in the writings of Marxists. Marxism was a compulsory subject in all schools. It was the unchallenged ideology of the state, propagated with every means of communication as the 'science of all sciences' and the 'art of all arts', to use the language of primary school books! For most students, Marxism was over-exposed, it had a strongly official sound. In the 'fifties, the official line was simplified into a Stalinist version of Marxism, as outlined in Stalin's pamphlet *Historical and Dialectical Materialism*. The majority of the people and particularly the young people developed a defence mechanism—they were plainly bored with Marxism!

This boredom was one of the reasons why the younger and keener Marxists reacted in the 'sixties in Czechoslovakia by developing new methods of teaching. They experimented with dialogue—with other philosophies and especially Christian philosophy. The discussion of Christian views appeared on the timetable of Marxist philosophy teachers. It was a total misunderstanding to label these teachers weak, or revisionist or relativist, as they were so labelled. The opposite was true. It was the keenest Marxists who saw that only by getting the study of Marxism out of the official ghetto could they interest their students. Only by setting Marxism against other world views and discussing its implications could they have any success at all. Unless they did this they were faced with a blank wall of indifference and obstinacy, despite, or perhaps because of, the official line. These teachers gave the theological faculty a great deal of trouble. We had to deal with a lack of interest among our students too. Without some effort on our part they would never have stood up to the 'informed' New Marxist students.

It was completely different in the West. When I was called to Basel in 1968 I thought that I would have to learn other philosophies, familiarize myself with

Existential Philosophy and Logical Positivism for my lectures on Systematic Theology. I soon discovered that this was not the case at all. A wave of interest in Marxism had swept over the schools of Western Europe. This was not universal, but clearly those students who were politically 'involved' or alert to the developments of culture in their own land were very interested in the encounter with Marxism. Marxist theory attracted them at once, they were completely open to the Marxist challenge, unfortunately often without reservations. I noticed at the theological faculty at Basel—and for that matter also later in Zurich and Paris—there were groups who assessed my lectures, not from the point of view of Christian theology, but with the practised Marxist eye. They would smile at criticisms of orthodox theological statements, but frown at any critical remark about Marxism.

This interest in Marxism pleased me, but I could not follow these students in their uncritical acceptance of Marxist 'orthodoxy'. No one who had been a citizen of a communist country could possibly accept Marxism like that, and I had theological reasons too. Experience of living in Czechoslovakia had cured me of belief in such slogans as 'the teaching of all teachings, the art of all arts'. Of course, one cannot blame Marxism for all the deformities of the 'fifties—as some anti-Marxists in east and west have done. There were too many 'unmarxist' components playing their part in the development of Stalinism, often consciously manipulating Marxist theory in the interest of Stalin's domestic and foreign policy. The historical development of Marxism has had its ambiguities and many of the doctrines of Marx and Lenin need periodic reconsideration.

I was disconcerted by the naîvety of these western students, so that I had repeatedly to call for a critical

13

attitude to Marxist history and theory. They seemed to ignore the experience of Eastern Europe, even though they had ample opportunity to consult people who had lived through these years of change. Such an attitude can be understood only as a defence mechanism in debate, where it may be necessary to combat the attitude of many in the West who are ready to point to defects as sufficient reason for dismissing Marxism. The fact that 'things are not as they should be' in Eastern Europe is too often used as a justification for the *status quo* in Western Capitalism, and as a global discrediting of Marxism. Communist attitudes may border on demagogy, but demagogy cannot be justified by another demagogy. A doctrinaire approach amounts to a flight from reality—and runs up against the best insights of Marxism itself—so that faced with the many-sided phenomenon of 'real Socialism' it is no longer able to be critical. Such a doctrinaire attitude is not possible for one who has been a citizen of a communist country.

But I also find an uncritical acceptance of Marxism without taking into account its variations quite impossible on theological grounds. Certainly, I consider Marxist philosophy to be a relevant and challenging possibility for modern theology, particularly in view of its penetrating and accurate analysis of social conditions. I am aware also of its closeness to the authentic teaching of the Bible. I shall spell this out later. But when I first met this total acceptance of the Marxist position and saw it built into systematic theology in its entirety, I could not accept it. Neither could I accept the Marxist way of thinking, with its unquestioned hypothesis, as suitable for Christian theology.

There are, at least, two reasons why I have difficulty with such total acceptance of the Marxist position into Christian theology:

First, on principle, it is my considered opinion that any

14

attempt to relate the Gospel too closely to an ideology is dangerous for its integrity and its identity;

Second, on practical grounds, that such an acceptance blurs the real difference between Marxism and Christianity—a situation which both sides must regard as undesirable.

For these two reasons, when I am asked if a Christian can be a Marxist, I have to say 'No!', when what is implied is a desire to hide the difference between the two ways of thinking and produce a 'blending into one'. But this refusal to accept a closed system into theology does not rule out an open acceptance into the theological enterprise of significant elements of Marxist theory, such as the materialistic and historical questioning of the church in history and at the present time. Neither does it rule out a practical and co-operative working between Marxists and Christians in concrete social tasks. I would rather affirm quite clearly that such co-operation is much easier because of a clear understanding.

Let me illustrate the need for a critical attitude to Marxist theory with an example—one of the central ideas of Marxism—the class struggle. In recent years one of the most 'involved' contemporary theologians in Germany, who has also shown himself most aware of Marxist thought, is Helmut Gollwitzer. He has energetically, at long last, persuaded his colleagues to put the Marxist theory on their agenda in Ethics and Dogmatics. He has convinced us that we must ourselves raise and critically examine the question of how the church's standing in society (which is always bound up with class) affects her teaching and practice.

I find this insistence by Gollwitzer, which is most clearly set out in his book *Die kapitalistiche Revolution* (1974), both important and overdue. For too long, these questions raised by theological reflection and practical experience have been excluded from the teaching of

Ethics and Philosophy. It is easy to see how this has happened. Theological studies have developed in recent years a whole series of critical movements—much as in science where the scene has also totally changed—in textual and historical criticism, in hermeneutics and the re-examination of literary sources. Compared with these studies, the critical examination of social conditions had a low priority.

A similar deficiency developed in traditional ethics. The old ethical concepts were under attack and there were no adequate theological tools to deal with new social problems. Theology became preoccupied and hesitant. How often, with side glances at Marxism, have Christians argued: 'The Christian concept is love of neighbour, not class struggle'? This will not do. It over-simplifies the way in which we take our ethical decisions; — they are always decisions taken with a given structure. Even when we are discussing Christian love, this structure cannot be ignored. Christian love is here taken to be more than a private sentimental happening, but the full sense of the Gospel's 'love of neighbour'. To follow this Gospel command of Jesus, to love our neighbour, is to ask about a real person and that question concerns the actual conditions under which that real person in a real community is required to live.

Undoubtedly, there has been a change in attitude to these matters in recent years. Since the Geneva conference on *Church and Society* (1966) we have learnt to speak more clearly of the 'love which shows itself through the structures'. The World Council of Churches has had to act upon these conclusions and as a result handle the protest that came from the churches. It is here that I see the theological and social importance of its *Programme to Combat Racism*. The churches are venturing far into the field of social ethics in their discussion with other groups. This departure from the traditional way of working is leading to radical statements by the churches—these awaken protest and reaction. Hence the need for a considerable reassessment of theology. It is precisely in this field that we meet the classical challenge of Marxist theory, i.e. its persistent questioning of social conditions and the system upon which they depend, or simply the class struggle. As theologians we have every reason to take this Marxist challenge seriously.

Our considerations must however be selective and critical. It would serve no purpose for the theologian to lean over backwards to accept the Marxist theory of the class struggle into his system uncritically. That would be foolish and irresponsible. There are at least three aspects of this theory which should be distinguished:

1. The Marxist indication that the life of man, historically and socially, is caused by frequently conflicting interests—haves and have-nots, privileged and under-privileged.

2. The Markist theory of this situation: the insistence upon the determinative influence of economics—and hence the need to draw up a programme for greater justice in economic terms.

3. The Marxist ideology of the class struggle: the identification of the class problem with the ownership of private property and the under-estimating of the other systems of authority and privilege, which can threaten even a socialist society. This becomes more important under the 'dictatorship of the proletariat' (as the experience of Eastern Europe has shown) with its monopoly of power and its ideological treatment of truth.

I have problems with this third aspect of Marxist theory, which is intimately bound up with the other two. The historical out-working of this theory requires

17

much closer examination. How often have the citizens of a socialist state, for example in Eastern Europe, been manipulated in the interests of a ruling élite, and with what tragic consequences! In our situation in Czechoslovakia, I think especially of Stalin's doctrine of the continuing, bitter class struggle. In its name, those who were ideologically different were branded as class enemies and liquidated—morally, professionally and, in extreme cases, physically. In the 'fifties, in almost every European country, by virtue of this theory, a scenario was written and the play performed. Admittedly, after the death of Stalin, Stalinism was (somewhat half-heartedly) recognized as a false development. The problem of the ideological theory of class struggle was not solved. Even in the late 'sixties there were still those who opposed every alteration in the *status quo,* every suggested change within the socialist state, including those changes which were in the direction of greater socialist democracy.

These experiences make one think. If we are to benefit from Marxist insights in church and theology then we must consider them critically. If we do, theology has a great deal to learn from the Marxist analysis of alienation in a capitalist society. For example we need to be cautious in the acceptance of the Marxist over-simplified answer to the question of the nature and 'place' of evil.

Old theological traditions could then become real again. I think of the much-maligned doctrine of sin which even theologians have often tended to put aside. According to this, evil has a multiple strategy in the world of men: it is not to be overcome or understood from one point of view, even the economic, however important. In order to throw back the powers of evil we need to develop a multiple strategy. To be plain: questions of the political, cultural and religious conditions cannot be treated as secondary in a (socialist) state. They must be never under-estimated or lost by absorption into economic problems. On this important point, Marxist theory and practice has so far refused to move.

There is no doubt that these questions have disturbed the politicians and the theoreticians in democratic socialsim. Take Willy Brandt as an example. In his latest book, he writes:

> Experience has shown that the realization of freedom for the individual is closely bound up with the problem of the right to own property. Experience has also shown that there can be a very close connection between collective economies and political dictatorships. On the other hand, a high degree of political, legal and social freedom has been achieved in more than one state without basic changes in the ownership of the means of production. Clearly, there is no automatic process by which 'socialization' or 'nationalization' inevitably brings more freedom to men.[1]

An assessment of these experiences is also important for theology. If a critical consideration is neglected now—and there are in the West pro-Marxist theologians, it seems to me, who are tempted to suppress these experiences—then a meaningful encounter with Marxism becomes a mockery. Such a phoney encounter would mean that the Marxists also would be left in the lurch by the theologians. Then the necessary critical attitude for dealing with any creative thought or action would be lacking—only the 'doctrinaire' (Marxist and Christian) would be happy. In the common interest of our contemporaries, who long for a humane change in church and society, we need an encounter which is both critical and open. This will be possible if each understands its need for the re-assessment of its own practice and theory, if each begins to move its own entrenched position. The movement is not sentimental and starry-eyed, but it will be in that direction described by the young Karl Marx in his memorable phrase 'to overthrow all situations in which men are degraded, enslaved, abandoned, despised'.[2]

1. From Anathema to Dialogue:

An Approach to The Christian-Marxist Movement

A Passing Fashion?

One of the most astounding developments in the cultural and social life of the late 'sixties was the conversation between Christians and Marxists. In a very short time it grew into a veritable explosion of interest on both sides in an encounter—in academic circles, East and West, but also in the mass gatherings after the events in Socialist Czechoslovakia in 1968. It has become the subject of many books and articles. A bibliography published by the World Council of Churches in Geneva in 1969, listing writings on this subject, gave more than a thousand titles. The dialogue grew until it really became a fashionable subject.

As with all popular themes, a critical question must be asked: Are we here concerned with anything more than a passing fashion, or is this a serious and meaningful undertaking? That question can be understood from the point of view of the cultural interaction: Christianity and Marxism are two comprehensive systems of thought and life. Both are relatively fixed, they have been discussed in every detail and tested. They are concerned with practically all areas of human thought and action. Can such established systems really have anything to learn from each other? Are they not both—by their implied or openly expressed universality—quite uninterested in alternative possibilities? Doesn't one exclude the other? Above all, their philosophical assumptions are very different, if not, as some of their theorists say on both sides, contradictory and totally irreconcilable.

Doubts grow when we look at the social situation in which any dialogue must take place, so remarkably different on each side. In the East of Europe, the Marxists are the dominant group—with all the privileges and institutional (often governmental) authority of a state ideology; while the Christians are advised to stay in the 'background'. In the West, it is Christendom— with a modified claim perhaps today—which holds the dominant position; while the Marxists appear to be the under-privileged. And so again, one must really ask: Under such conditions is it possible to come to a real encounter? Isn't this discussion doomed from the outset to be 'lame', an unequal conversation, ambiguous and perhaps dishonourable? Are there not more barriers than bonds here?

These objections must be taken seriously. And yet, I am convinced of the significance of this experiment. I must add at once that while I am convinced of the possibility, I am fully aware of the difficulties. It is not at all self-evident that it will succeed. There is no precedent to encourage me in history and no evidence of success in the present. This is a dangerous and unstable undertaking, always 'extraordinary' and risky. To have any illusions about this would be pure cloud cuckoo land.

One historical consideration may sober us. It is

somewhat local, but it was a dialogue: the late 'sixties was the period of this experiment, and the year 1968 marked—in East and West—both its high point and its destruction. Since then we can trace a falling off in interest. Today, there is no lack of voices which speak already of the 'death of dialogue'. It is noticeable that such judgements come from the right and from the left. From the right: with clear confidence, the conservatives and the dogmatists of Marxism and Christianity, declare the end of dialogue. They trace the disturbance caused by that encounter in church and party. With some reason now they can say, 'See, it doesn't work'. Then the general guideline for the future is, 'Prevent it from starting!' No wonder that the protagonists of dialogue on both sides were dealt with severely. In France one has the example of the Garaudy affair among the communists, and Girardi on the Catholic side.

There are also critical comments coming from the left. 'Dialogue is dead', writes the left-wing Austrian Catholic Günther Nenning, who was himself earnestly engaged earlier in dialogue. Similar radical voices are heard from other 'involved' Catholics and Marxists. They question the consequences of the shattering of dialogue, they try to explain this by saying that talking is not enough—what is needed is joint action! When they are engaged in this they soon discover that Christians and Marxists come much closer than was possible in dialogue. Above all a serious working together with Marxists can bring both sides to an understanding, as Marx himself has said in a classic formula: 'The weapons of criticism cannot put right . . . the criticism of the weapons'.[3] Already in his day it was necessary to warn against attaching too much importance to arguments and dialogue—particularly in the German culture!

I take this criticism from the left very seriously.

23

The left knows the danger of every dialogue: that it might degenerate into uncommitted talk. The danger was recognized by those who took part in the dialogue, from the beginning: the dialogue in Czechoslovakia was anything but an uncommitted game, as it is sometimes still designated. Nonetheless, we can hardly deny that there is a temptation to engage in dialogue as criticism. But this does not justify what I would call the more dangerous temptation: to undervalue the cultural discussion. The need to reflect and to exchange one's thought with the other side is more than the private concern of the notorious intellectuals: it is a vital concern of every healthy society—also and especially for a socialist society. Side by side with that quote from Marx we must put its dialectical counterpoint. Then it seems to me that we shall come closer to an understanding of the great dialectician: 'The criticism of the weapons cannot put right the weapons of criticism'. An attack on the weapons can hinder the development of a dialogue but it can never destroy it. Those who talk of the death of dialogue should consider this fact.

We cannot pronounce dialogue as a dangerous experiment which has failed on the basis of what followed; we need to look further back and see what was there before the dialogue was attempted. That situation was already difficult. When one considers the century or more of co-existence between Marxism and Christianity in European political and cultural history, it is quite clear that there was practically no dialogue at all between these two great schools of thought. Instead there was enmity, confrontation and usually an attempt to destroy each other. Anathema, not dialogue, marked this co-existence.

It is not too much to say that the persistent refusal of these two embittered houses to enter into dialogue went against the best interests of both. I am thinking

24

here not only of the undeniable common ground between Christianity and Marxism (of which much will be said in this book) but rather that common need of dialogue in both families. Both are dialectic and 'eccentric'. They both know that the world we men have fashioned is a dynamic process. And they both know that therefore the way to understand this world of men and to get at the truth by way of encounter or meeting. So they are conscious, because they both accept the nickname 'eccentric', that their own way of thinking, their own system of knowledge and faith, cannot be self-evident. They both know that they must strive beyond themselves towards a reality which is greater than their system. It is in being true to these basic themes in their own traditions that both creative Christians and creative Marxists should turn towards dialogue.

Yet—this is not what is happening. In both houses other tendencies are at work. Both have their times and areas of rigidity and dogmatic exclusiveness. In the paradoxical situations which have developed, both have allowed themselves to become prisoners of the class- and power-politics of the systems from which they benefit. One has only to think of the period of the cold war—and the misuse of Christianity (and of Marxism) in that unhappy situation, when a dangerous 'crusader' mentality was nourished.

The way 'from anathema to dialogue', with such an historical legacy, is bound to be long and difficult. But it must be tried—first by individuals in both camps, then by whole groups. In what follows I would like to give a short report of a stretch of the way. I think particularly of that 'stretch' in which I have myself played a part and the things that happened on the road: the Czechoslovakia road.

Beginning and Growth of a Readiness for Dialogue

Our first years as Christians and Marxists living together in a socialist state (after 1964) were marked by that atmosphere which we have already described as typical of European 'co-existence': mistrust and mutual defensiveness. both sides remained in their trenches and behind protective walls. Each side talked with the other in monologue, whether critically or apologetically. The rare occasions for an exchange of views led only to a confrontation. Both sides gave good reasons for their entrenched positions, revealing by these reasons their own ideological stereotype and their inflexible attitudes to each other. Many Christians had been taught that Marxists were atheists and materialists, and they interpreted this as sufficient grounds for describing them as enemies of religion and of morality. And almost all Marxists saw Christians as obstacles to progress and enlightenment.

Under such circumstances, meeting was impossible until something had been done to defuse the ideologies. To borrow an awkward word from theology and make it more awkward—both had to be de-mythologized or de-ideologized. Don't misunderstand that word. It does not mean a radical condemnation of all ideology. German theology, in particular, in its treatment of Marxism, tried that unprofitable way for a few years after the War. It got nowhere. Ideology plays an important role in the life of man and the society he builds: it can clarify common experience, gather common strength. At the same time the temptation is always there, to make the ideology absolute. If this is done, problems are over-simplified, social reality is never clearly seen. Above all, such absolutizing of an ideology destroys the image of our fellow man as our neighbour. An absolute ideology makes understanding impossible; it does not unite, but manipulates.

In a situation so drunk with ideology as Czechoslovakia in the 'fifties, how could one think of de-ideologizing? Very little could be expected from Marxism in those days of Stalin's rigid dogmatism. For this very reason it became most important for us Christians—at least from our side—to keep open the way to true dialogue. Some of us tried to do this in the darkest days of doctrinaire Stalinism. Not all Christians were ready. Understandably, the majority were inclined to answer monolithic Marxism with their own monolithic Christianity. christian apologetics was used to oppose the possible inroads of Marxism with a strong theology—a theology, or ideology, of separatism. We owe it to our theological teacher, J. L. Hromádka, that the majority did not prevail! At least in theological circles a much more open attitude to Marxism was maintained.

The task of opening up ways to true dialogue had two sides. First, to understand what Marxism really was in its initiative and deeper possibilities. Admittedly, the official Stalin-Marxist line did not encourage such an attempt. But especially here it was important for us not to confuse the given ideological teaching with the real possibilities of Marxism. In other words we must de-ideologize the Stalin version of Marxism and search for its humane and original form.

In different ways we attempted this. We concentrated our studies particularly on the young Karl Marx. It is not perhaps without interest to record that the Christians undertook this study before the Marxists did! Some of us were already acquainted with the work of the Swiss theologian Franz Lieb, who had studied the texts of the young Karl Marx and pointed out their theological and political relevance. And so it came about in the early 'fifties that the Comenius Faculty in the University of Prague was probably the first to undertake a study of this philosophy first as a challenge to theology and the church, and then also to Stalin's

27

form of Marxism. This effort was in no way directed against the Marxists, mounting an apologetic or ideological struggle, but the contrary. It was intended to help Marxists understand their origins better, or rather to help us both, and that was very important, towards a more human face for our socialist society and in this way to lead to our future dialogue.

An even greater importance was seen in the other aspect of de-ideologizing. This was the concentrated effort to build a new reality into Christian thought and action, so that by a 'demonstration of power and the spirit' some of the obstacles to Christianity for the intelligent Marxist could be seen to be removed. In this way the traditional Marxist image of Christianity was also de-ideologized.

What is meant by this? According to the traditional Marxist interpretation, religion is either superstition or an instrument to justify class privilege. (We shall be concerned with various aspects of the Marxist theory of religion in this book). This accusation is put by Marx in different ways, but it always tends towards this double attack. It is understandable when we consider the role played by the church at the time of the development of Marxist thought. As a concrete and historical thinker, his political philosophy naturally reflects this. In view of this we must admit that his critical views are largely justified. The church was and remained, a conservative and reactionary force. But this means that the church still has no chance today, particularly in a socialist society, to meet this criticism effectively so long as she incorporates a spirit of superstition and reactionary political thought. If she cannot 'put her house in order' in this sense she may call for an ideological crusade, she may engage in apologetics on a wide front and thereby in many ways withstand the accusations of Marxism—but she will have no success, because she remains unconvincing. A credibility gap opens up between us which cannot be bridged by assertions and explanations, however correct they may be.

A real encounter with Marxist theory requires of us that we make a determined effort to close this sorry gap, so that the true condition and the practical life of the church may call in question the stereotyped expectations of Marxist theory. That includes two major concerns:

1. The temptation to superstition, which is so often equated with human aspirations to religion, must be tackled by the development of a critical theology. This is obviously not easy at a time when the church is under attack from outside. A persecuted church tends to take up a defensive and self-justifying position, which, humanly speaking, is fully understandable. One exaggerates and lays hold on every possible method to retain what one has. Understandable, but from the point of view of communicating with a hostile world, quite useless. Instead of communication the church develops very quickly a fundamentalistic 'ghetto mentality'.

The 'Prague theology' energetically resisted this tendency. We were helped by our past—the socially involved Hussite Reformation—and encouraged by the hope of communicating with our Socialist colleagues. Both helped us, in the Comenius Faculty particularly, to develop a quite different emphasis in our theology from the conservative, fundamentalist direction. The questions of the secular world—not only Marxist—could not easily be set aside. The ecumenical de-mythologizing debate was taken up critically, and openly, particularly in the writings of the well-known New Testament scholar, J. B. Souček. The most important theological work, significantly initiated by the laity and pressed by the congregations, was the development of a new kind of preaching. The attempt was made with great enthusiasm to devise a 'reasonable preaching', which would be adapted to the situation of secularized man. The intensive theological work of the Faculty and the lively spiritual condition of the congregations made it very difficult for the doctrinaire Marxist to continue to speak of the Protestant churches as a 'hotbed of superstition'.

2. The other more important task was related to the Marxist thesis, that religion is to be understood as the class ideology of the privileged. It was necessary to show that this was not the whole truth about the Christian churches—and to show it once again, not by declarations, but by the quality of life of the Christian congregations. For this reason it was most important that the churches should not pronounce an unqualified disapproval of all that had happened since 1948. Admittedly the Communist victory and subsequent developments since had caused great difficulties for the churches as for many other groups in the country. It was not possible to give an unqualified approval either. But a bitter sense of righteous indignation must not so dominate the churches' attitude to Communism and all that it has brought to Czechoslovakia, so that the impression is given of a total rejection. That would be to present the churches in the light of having only a negative relation to the principles of Socialism. The radical structural changes brought with them not only loss, but opportunities. This must be thoroughly recognized by the Christians, particularly in the hope that these socialist opportunities might be grasped and used to build up a happy human society. It must be made clear that the Christians are not obsessed by the privileges they have lost, but rather by the new tasks to which they are called in the building up of a just society. By taking part in these new tasks, Christians are not compromising or selling their birthright, but faithful to their true motivation: the biblical message. This means that the continuance of an intact Christian

presence in the midst of a socialist society demonstrates by example that the 'Christian religion' can in no way be identified with a reactionary ideology.

It is more difficult to formulate these tasks in general concepts. It was much more difficult to put them into practice in the daily life of the church. Quite frankly it didn't always happen. It is not too much to say, however, that at least in some places the contours of a new reality became visible in the 'fifties, which did not fit the Marxist stereotype of the church. It was scarcely possible to characterize the Christian congregations any longer as gatherings of old-fashioned and unenlightened people. It was also quite obviously wrong to see the churches as 'breeding grounds for the reactionaries'. There were no more privileges to be won by a Christian living openly in a Socialist society. The contrary was true. A Christian had more often to fear a subtle or deliberate discrimination from the official side. Any idea of opportunism which had often been true of the church in the past, was gone. The church, and with her also theology, had a unique and growing opportunity, amidst all the losses she had suffered. She had the chance of a new credibility. This above all else would be important for her future dialogue with Marxists.

It was a long time before the first contact with the Marxist in any kind of dialogue was made. The quiet invitation was not heard at first, because both sides were too taken up with their own concerns. The churches were defending their theological and ecclesiastical positions. The Marxists were not at first disposed to take too seriously the churches' changes. One could explain such changes all too easily as they were thought to be conclusively adaptations of the churches, now thanks to the socialist society, with their backs to the wall, trying to sing the socialist song. It is of no great significance to be progressive when there is nothing else left to do! Or there were the other explanations: progressive Christians feel sympathetic, but basically they are split personalities. It was in this way that Milan Machovec, later a protagonist and pioneer of a Christian-Marxist dialogue, himself tried to explain at first the attitude of J. L. Hromádka. He was a progressive man, he said, despite his Christianity. At this stage, the idea that a Christian could play a positive role in a socialist society because of his Christianity was not yet taken seriously.

The realization of dialogue, however, brought about some changes in 'the other camp', among Marxists. That became evident first about the end of the 'fifties, when a noticeable change of direction occurred in Czech culture. Restless and creative young Marxists began to see new problems. They had been totally loyal during the profound changes in society and culture; but now the fundamental changes in our society and its structure, necessary to build a socialist state, had been accomplished. Property and means of production had almost totally changed hands. The Marxist-Socialist foundation was firmly laid: the house of the new society was built. But what about the new man in this new house? The question of man was posed with a new and unavoidable urgency.

This question had seemed unimportant in the first years after 1948. Stalin's orthodoxy dismissed it as typically bourgeois. So the question of man was subordinated to the problem of changing the structure of society. One of the official slogans of the time was 'The end of all our striving is Man'. But in fact this 'the end' was in a very real sense ambiguous. 'End' can mean 'aim' or chronologically, when all else has been done, 'at the end'. And very often it meant putting the question of man in brackets and leaving it until the end to be discussed.

This tendency to displace the problem of man was strengthened by typical Marxist assumptions. It was

32

assumed that by changing the economic base, all the problems of the superstructure would be solved, including problems of ethics and personal life. it was at this point that the young Marxists posed their questions: Is it possible to leave out the question of man? The structural alterations in the foundation have largely been realized. Is it not high time that the problems of man were urgently faced? what is the meaning of life? What is the purpose of history—and not only the universal historical process, but my personal history? Can individuals, even whole generations, be satisfied with the answer, that the coming communist society will bring its own solution for these things? And what about the question of evil? Has one solved the riddle of evil once the structure of society has been revolutionarily changed and a new social order built? Or another problem: Can one ignore the question of truth in face of the official teaching of the party? Is it enough simply to accept and await the explanation of the party when faced by the grim realities of a political trial? Is the call: 'Comrades, believe the party' really a satisfactory answer for the party member?

The questions were real and insistent. One had to come to grips with them. the first publications—like the booklet by Milan Machovec on the meaning of life—soon became best-sellers. Then came stimulus from the other socialist countries, like Poland. the philosophy of man once again became a real concern. The Marxists attempted to develop this philosophy from their own, original tradition. That meant the rediscovery of the stimulating and disturbing thought of the young Karl Marx, particularly his *Economical and Philosophical Manuscripts* of 1844. At the heart of this whole discussion arose the concept of alienation. Is this Marxist concept valid also for a socialist society? And if it is still valid, as appears more and more obvious, how is it to be interpreted and what must be done with it?

In this connection, non-Marxist thought and philosophy proved important. Existentialism, which for years had been condemned and ignored as typically decadent writing from a burgeois culture, was seriously studied. Attention was also directed towards those parts of modern literature and poetry which dealt with the problem of evil, which described the rootless situation of man in the twentieth century and his new possibilities and new dangers. Franz Kafka was rediscovered—with all his problems; questions about the fate of man and the alienated relationships of institutional manipulation. The struggle flared up: are the 'kafka situations' simply to be identified with the capitalist society and its technocracy? Or is there some evidence that these dangers can be recognized also in the central structure of a socialist society, with its overbearing party bureaucracy? It was typical that in this inter-national discussion of the theme, the Czech thinkers responded positively to the challenging questions, while the representatives of German ideology in the German Democratic Republic dismissed them dogmatically.

Did this new cultural ferment bring with it also a new closeness to the Christian tradition? Not at once and not directly. That came with some hesitation and after much thought. That was understandable. For a Marxist, a theological answer to the question of man would be seen as a confusion of the issue, or as an illegitimate answer. Despite this, some classical themes of Christian theology re-appeared on the horizon of these young Marxist thinkers: the problem of personal identity and ultimate integrity; the question of guilt and sin; the phenomenon of prayer and much else beside. These themes were no longer considered to be totally irrelevant or 'meaningless' trivia. That was certainly a very important change and it opened up from the Marxist

34

side a possibility of meeting and exchange of ideas between Christians and Marxists.

If I was asked to point to the most important changes in this attitude of the new Marxists, I would say that it was the discovery of the biblical tradition. This tradition had been pushed into the background during the early days of the socialist society. Much of the propaganda in the name of the 'cultural revolution' had been for the extermination of Christian thinking, or at least silencing it. The spiritual and cultural consequences of this were sad—also for the Marxist. They lost contact with the prophetic tradition which meant so much to Karl Marx. In particular they lost the insights into history as a dynamic, meaningful process, which was not yet ended and was still open. And as a result, they also lost a deeper understanding of the question of man. Thus, much was lost of the original creative power of Marxism, allowing the static and dogmatic elements to dominate, so that the official Marxism surrendered a great deal of its power to attract.

In the 'sixties, this situation had basically altered. Some Marxists discovered the originality of biblical thought and its real importance for their own thinking, which had been formed by the scientific positivism of a 19th-century view of the world. The biblical stream of Western thought was thus seen to be culturally valuable and important. In this way, a ripple of interest in the Bible and Christian tradition was set up.

Perhaps the best example was the stimulating series of articles which appeared in 1967 in a leading literary journal in Prague, *Literární noviny*. They appeared later in book form and aroused an even greater interest. This was the work by V. Gardavský, with the meaningful title, *God is not quite dead*. This was a critical, but very understanding treatment of biblical thought, making the point that the biblical inheritance has much to say to socialist culture and society. This understanding and recognition brought with it an assumption that the meeting between Marxism and Christianity, the concrete discussion between Marxists and Christians, is not empty illusion. It is only in the interest of human development within the socialist state when citizens, committed to Marxism and Christian convictions, meet in open exchange of views. The dialogue is possible and necessary.

This breakthrough to dialogue was both deepened and broadened by a similar development in international discussion. On the Christian side the change had been considerable. The Second Vatican Council and the World Council of Churches showed great changes in their attitude to Marxism. The step from anathema to dialogue was decided upon, even though, so far, it had not been ventured. And the Communist parties, especially in the west, sought contact with their fellow-citizens in new ways. This was particularly true in Italy and in France. And so dialogue was arranged in many places, in a European context.

Of course, most important for the Czech Christians and Marxists were the meetings in their own context, in their own society. This developed very happily, not only at the universities, where opportunities for dialogue had existed for many years, e.g. at Charles University in Prague, where under the leadership of Milan Machovec, a continuous stream of philosophers and theologians had met at regular intervals. Not only there but also, very soon, in a much wider setting, at mass gatherings as in Prague in April, 1968. It was not until the invasion by military powers from outside that the organized dialogue was ended. That invasion put democracy on trial.

Mutual Questioning
We have so far tried to describe the way to dialogue.

What is the continuing significance of this way? What was and what is the meaning of this discussion? There are many possible answers to this question. Personally, I would take as one of the most important aspects of the dialogue which has so far emerged, the phenomenon of 'mutual questioning'. The phrase is taken from the French Marxist Roger Garaudy, who used it to rescue the debate from the blind alley of the kind of dialogue that was getting nowhere. There can be unfruitful discussions. There are 'dialogues of the dumb'—mock conversations which begin with pre-conceived ideas and follow through to the confirmation of pre-determined positions, unable to hear any other note than their own. Or, at least as often, 'the conversation of kindred spirits', which covers over the deepest differences in theory and practice with idealization and phoney agreement. Neither of these two kinds of discussion is of any real value. There is value only in a critical and open encounter in the setting of common responsibility, and that also in the face of one's own tradition, in the light of common practical tasks. Unless both can do this a meaningful dialogue cannot develop from the encounter.

For my part, I would see the first hope of any meaningful dialogue in the questioning of my tradition by my colleague, who by his particular, and to me strange, emphasis can challenge the notorious, and therefore easily overlooked, temptations and assumptions of my own tradition.

Every spiritual movement is in danger of standing for one particular programme and one particular way of looking at the world. In the course of its history, it will attempt to fix this particular view dogmatically— if not to fossilize it! Specific emphases are seen no longer as emphases, but as firmly grounded positions. In this way the various aspects of its original dynamic and flexible attitude become stylized. So long as this dogmatic stylizing is related to the original movement and can be questioned, no harm is done. As in all historical movements, the questioning keeps it alive and brings out a relatively new contemporary view. The danger comes with the fixing of a 'dogmatic orthodoxy', which fails to communicate with the outside world—and equally with its own origins. Then any philosophy or theology stagnates. As opposed to this there is the possibility of an honourable dialogue. When we listen to the 'strange' questioning, we recognize our own one-sidedness, and, under favourable conditions, even the 'stylizing' of our own inheritance.

What can such a 'mutual questioning' between Marxists and Christians mean in real terms? Here again I would like to use a formulation by Roger Garaudy. The special work of the Marxist is to remind the Christian of the reality of historical and social immanence. And the special gift of the Christian is to be able to show to the Marxist the importance of the dimension of transcendence for personal and social life.

I am convinced that such a mutual learning has already taken place. I have been astonished at the extent of these dialogues and at the reactions they have produced among many important thinkers on both sides. In the following chapters of this book I will be taking up several concrete themes. Here I confine myself to the assessment of a very important occasion of dialogue in the 'sixties: the Symposium at Mariánské Lázne (Marienbad) in 1967. This occasion was particularly important because it was organized by the predominantly Christian and Western-orientated *Society of Paul* together with the *Czech Academy of Science*. This made it possible to bring together a truly representative, a truly European conference of Marxists and Christians.

Any who thought of Christianity as a kind of

metaphysical or a private affair must have been disturbed by the presentations given by the theologians at Marienbad. There were quite different emphases in their expositions. First, there was the insistence upon the historical and social life of man. This was most evident in the paper given by the Catholic theologian Johannes B. Metz. In his presentation, he passionately denounced Christianity for its retrograde step back to concentration upon the private area of life, as is clearly observed in theology since the Enlightenment. In the exposition of the Bible, for example, modern, bourgeois theologians worked above all with the categories of personality and the inner life. The social implications of the faith were downgraded as 'secondary' or 'derived'. Living faith found itself primarily in the sphere of personal 'I-Thou' relations.

This tendency must now be reversed. To neglect the social context of man means to lose sight of his concrete existence and therefore of his true personality. It is no longer possible to think of existence in the modern world apart from the given structures, social and historical, which are deeply embedded in this world. And such thinking would be biblical! The central affirmations of the Bible cannot be narrowed down to the private sphere. The eschatological promises—freedom, peace, justification, reconciliation—all have a 'social dimension', which calls for a corresponding action. If the church hears this call aright, she will become an 'Institution for the constructive criticism of society'. Otherwise, in a very real part of her life, she will become salt that has lost its savour.

This theological stress on the social responsibility of the church is closely bound up with another emphasis. The church must be understood in a dynamic sense. She must reckon with a possibility—in fact, necessity—of radical change in this modern world. There can be situations in which taking part in a revolution is the consequence of Christian love. Giulio Girardi, another Catholic theologian, laid out openly at Marienbad his *Theses on Revolution*. The traditional condemnation of revolution, which by and large is the overwhelming attitude of Christian social ethics, must be overcome and different criteria developed for the 'boundary situations' in society.

A third emphasis which I would like to note is that of the 'church-centred' attitude, which both Catholic and Protestant theologians attempted to overcome. This was one of the main points stressed by Jürgen Moltmann in his paper on *The Theology of Hope*. The 'Hope' which the Christian proclaims is biblical and as such is not confined to the inner life of the church. It is not the hope of religion and its survival, but the hope of the kingdom of God, as the future of the world. The church cannot take to herself privileges which she denies to others. Freedom, for example, which is understood simply as religious freedom is a limited, if not a perverted, form of freedom.

I don't think it is too much to say that these three emphases were recognized by all the theologians who took part in the Marienbad conference as important, despite the very real differences of theology and confession among them. And these elements are placed high in Marxist thinking. Traditionally these have been points of conflict between Christians and Marxists. This seems to indicate that the questions put by Marxists to Christians have not found only deaf ears, nor fallen on unfruitful ground.

Now let us give our attention to the Marxists. Can we establish a corresponding 'reciprocal response' in their thinking? Let us go back a bit to our earlier thoughts: in this case, should not the dialectical questioning of the reasons for transcendence be given greater importance and at the same time a discriminating attention given to problems of Church and

Religion. In this area, particularly among dogmatic circles, there is a need for a reconsideration of Marxist attitudes so far. There were in fact traces of this happening in a number of Marxist papers.

First in the *Problem of Transcendence*. The new situation with regard to this so far neglected problem is evidenced particularly in the contributions of the Czech Marxists. Milan Prucha, for example, in his lecture made a notable attempt to gain consent for a new Marxist approach to the question of man. He did this against the background of the classical philosophical problem of 'Being'. Prucha attacked the view that the anthropological problem can be reduced to the historical and the social dimensions of human life. Of course, man is an historical and social being, as Marxism has not ceased to say on every possible occasion; but these important dimensions—and this Marxism has not always clearly seen—do not represent the total reality of human life. In this connection the question of true transcendence is posed. Prucha answered it with reference to the concept of 'Being'. The fundamental reality must not be too quickly determined either by the concept of material (as in traditional materialism) not by the concept of God (as in the religious tradition). In this way, Prucha launched an attack on theology from an unexpected quarter. He confessed that in the course of the Christian-Marxist conversations 'our Christian friends have awakened in us the taste and the appetite for transcendence'. But a question must be thrown back on the Christians, to be rethought and sharpened. The Christians are not yet ready to present the transcendence problem in its true depth. They hesitate to define transcendence with particularity. They describe it in such a way that transcendence is defined by the concept of 'God'. The philosopher must reject this step. Prucha had raised a critical question on this theological thesis, which

41

required an answer, but the question is of a different kind from that which Marxists have raised in the past. No longer does the Marxist think of the whole area of questioning about transcendence as an illusion. He takes it seriously. In the future it will not be possible to 'harness' the idea of transcendence to Christian sentimentality, but in the face of such philosophical questions it will be set free from its religious fetters.

This unexpected change in the traditional confrontation between Christians and Marxists in philosophy was not the only development. There was also a new emphasis in the Marxist theory of religion. This happened on many sides—especially in the lecture by Robert Kalivoda. The Marxist historian and philosopher from Czechoslovakia rejected as a deplorable misunderstanding the assumption that the sentence by Marx on religion as opium of the people (which we were much concerned with) was an adequate statement of Marxist theory of Christianity. It is in principle wrong to build a Marxist doctrine upon a classical question, usually taken out of its context. Such types of Marxist thinking are long past. Marxism is the discovery of the dialectic of the historical and social reality.

In the same way a Marxist theory, and this applies also to a Marxist theory of Christianity, must be tested. This means: when Christianity has provided the exclusive and unchallenged view of the world in Europe for more than a thousand years, it cannot simply be dismissed as only opium. In fact, the history of Europe is dialectic, not linear. And Christianity also has played a dialectical role. Undoubtedly, it has served as an opium, as ideological support for the social and political interests of the ruling class, which was often the church herself. But in its original form, it was in fact a revolt against the injustices of this world and then it played a progressive role. This can be seen most clearly in the revolutionary streams of Christian non-conformity, e.g. the Hussites. Because of this the Marxist needs to move towards an encounter with Christians to work out in analysis and dialectically a new theory of religion, vis-à-vis Christianity.

According to my understanding, the new approach by the Marxists expressed in these new emphases was in no way a few voices crying in the wilderness. The majority of the Marxists at Marienbad supported this new approach. Once again, we can say that the 'mutual questioning', which we had noted from the side of the Christians, in the theological work of the last decade and above all by the concerned attitude towards the church herself and in the ecumenical movement, such questioning has *not* so far as Marxists are concerned fallen on deaf ears. Here too the dialogue has a new start.

Eccentricity of the Dialogue

The progress of the Marxist-Christian discussion has brought real disturbances and new discoveries to both traditions. how are we to assess these changes? Do we see here a general philosophical muddle, in which clearly differentiated positions can no longer be determined and no one knows any more 'who is who'? Does the discussion lead at last to an amorphous mass of half-Christian Marxism related to a half-Marxist Christianity?

There are those who assess the value of the dialogue in this way. These are concerned with the integrity of their own position. But to see the conversation in this way is to misunderstand it. Mutual questioning leads in the opposite direction. Dialogue means challenge. The differences are not ironed out, but much more clearly defined. Much is achieved because we are not concerned here with a mutual ignoring, but rather with a mutual challenge in the form of questions. Listening to critical questions raised by colleagues does not lead to a betrayal of one's own tradition. Because theologians can now accept those three relatively new emphases put before them by Marxists does not mean that they have replaced the Bible by *Das Kapital*. And because Marxists take the question of transcendence more seriously, or because they discover that 'God is not quite dead', does not mean that they have given up their critical attitude to religion. Under the pressure of dialogue with each other a process of renewal is set in motion by which each studies again its own creative possibilities and makes new discoveries. The living spirit of both traditions can be awakened out of the sleep of dogmatism. Many of us who have taken part in the Christian-Marxist discussion are thankful for the experience of this possibility. This remains—even though today the institutional form of the dialogue has been shattered.

There is but one further dimension of dialogue. Let us recall what we said at the beginning of our discussion: Christianity and Marxism are not only dialectical ways of life and thinking—they are both 'eccentric'. That is meant literally—'out from the centre'. They do not have their centre in themselves, they are not their own objective. The impulse itself which has led them to new encounters leads both of them necessarily outside themselves. In the long run neither of them can be content to remain the theme of the other's discussion. Mutual questioning opens up further horizons of joint responsibility. It was no accident that the Christian-Marxist dialogue in Czechoslovakia opened up more than the practical question of co-existence in a socialist state, in which the Marxist laboured successfully for a just cultural policy. But both began to recognize a joint responsibility for a third party. To be precise, the problems of 'the third world' were more sharply focussed. This is inevitable. A real dialogue develops well beyond concern with one's own affairs. The best insights of both traditions lead to a truly 'ecumenical' view.

Today as never before we are faced with the possibilities of destruction or new creation. More than ever before we have to think responsibility and act carefully in the face of a question of survival for mankind. Not all contemporary movements are conscious of this. Neither is every philosophical and cultural tradition, and certainly not the somewhat amorphous understanding of life in our superficial, consumer society, of both east and west. The tendency to look back to private interests, to consumer attitudes and—most dangerous of all—fatalism, appears to be gaining the upper hand in our society.

Here, I would see one of the most important opportunities for a dialogue between Christians and Marxists. Let us have no illusions about the range of this discussion. Possibly, we are talking about two small minorities—but in no way depressed minorities. We must not overlook the fact that while the two families have many differences, they have also many common tasks. Both have been concerned and said much about the universe, about nature. Both have much to do still in this direction. Both have critical questions to put, as indeed the biological humanists have also. These two minorities do not offer a simple solution for the survival of man.

Yet, these two groups from the deepest motives of their respective traditions reject fatalism and indifference and accept their responsibility for history, and hopefully also for nature. They differ in the motives for their involvement and in the ultimate purpose of their hope. They speak different and sometimes contradictory languages. Their strategies are different. But both live—in so far as they live authentically— both live in the knowledge of an obligation to act responsibly. When the questions are put from these different points of view and something is contributed from each tradition, then the discussion cannot be meaningless or remain without significance—not even for those who are outside both camps.

2. The Image of Man in the Young Karl Marx :

A Question to Christians and Marxists

The most important breakthrough in the difficult path from 'anathema to dialogue' came when the Marxists concerned themselves with the problem of man. Turning their attention to the 'philosophy of man' was closely tied up with the spiritual hunger of the Marxist society of the 'fifties. Until that point the question of the meaning of human life had been subordinated to structural problems. The change came with the publication—and it was truly a publishing event—of *Economic and Philosophical Manuscripts* and other works of the young Karl Marx.

These manuscripts were first prepared by Marx in 1844 during his exile in Paris, but had remained unpublished. They were first published nearly 90 years later in 1932, but still remained relatively unknown. The atmosphere of the age of Stalin's 'orthodoxy' was not favourable to this work of the young Marx. It was looked upon as a first draft, concerned mostly with criticism of Hegel's philosophy and an early attempt to deal with political economy. Here, according to the judgement of orthodoxy, was an immature work. What this meant—at least on first consideration—was that it was fragmentary, a first sketch, which Marx himself was not particularly pleased with.

This was, however, only one side of the picture. The other side concerned the subject matter. The 'fragments' dealt with the subject of the fate of man in a dehumanizing system of social relationships. This undertaking was a personal and profound venture into the history of European humanism. Above all, this theme and this approach was suspect by the Stalin regime. As far as possible it was left officially in the shadows of neglect. That was why it first came to be studied by theologians, rather than Marxists. In 1961 it was first published in a Czech translation and soon became of crucial concern to the young philosophers. At once it provided a basis for a Christian-Marxist dialogue. Its theme—the philosophy of man—and its setting in the tradition of European humanism, both clearly understood, provided a unifying contact. This theme, dealt with in the concrete terms of man's social and cultural need, made an immediate appeal both to the young Marxists and to the Christians. And the context of the young Karl Marx within humanism made mutual understanding easier than the rigid schoolroom of Stalin's orthodoxy.

We shall attempt to define the real contours of the Marxist view of man and its importance for the Christian-Marxist dialogue, through a study of the Paris text, with some references to other writings by Marx.

Alienated Labour

At the centre of the economic and philosophical analysis of the young Karl Marx stands the social phenomenon of alienated labour. Under this heading two concepts were developed which must be explored if we are to understand the Marxist image of man. In what direction do they point?

1. The philosophy of Marx is basically a philosophy of work. There is no other movement in the history of philosophy or social studies which concerns itself with the problem of human labour with anything like the same intensity as does Marxism. That is easily recognized in the mature and clearly expressed form of his analysis. The emphasis on work is what is specific about Marxist economy: labour is the only source of commercial wealth. Work also plays a key role in anthropology, as it does in an anthropological book by Friedrich Engels, clearly expressed in the title: *The Part played by Labour in the Humanizing of Apes.* Labour creates the authentic human world. It is the true *officina humanitatis,* the factory bench of humanity.

This constructive element of Marxist thought is already fully developed in the young Marx. The extent to which their philosophy takes the subject of labour seriously became the decisive touchstone for Marx's attitude to his philosophical teachers and contemporaries. the high value he placed upon the philosophy of Hegel, despite considerable reservations about his idealism, is basically for this reason. Hegel's philosophy grasped something of the decisive role of labour. On the same basis, he broke with Feuerbach, despite continuing gratitude for his materialistic criticism of religion, precisely because of this. Feuerbach's static materialism could not do justice to the 'objective activity' of man.

Why is labour so decisively important for the theoretical and practical understanding of man? Marx gives an answer to this question at various levels. The highest of these levels concerns the 'place of man in the universe'. Labour is the true answer to man's environment, the situation given by nature. Man is bound to nature by his labour. It is impossible to think of his life without the background of a material universe—the world of objects with which he may and must work. At the same time, in the process of work, Nature is bound up with man, its abstract objectivity determined and taken up into history. In this way labour is a bridge, from both sides, across the chasm between subject and object, mediating and reconciling man and the universe. It is in man's labour that he and the world of nature achieve a common purpose. 'For the *"socialist"* man, what is called world history is none other than the product of human labour and the development of nature for man'.[4]

On the human scale, one can hardly place labour higher than that. For a theologian it reads like eschatology or *Heilsgeschichte* (redemption history) and gives to labour a function in these terms. Within the context in which Marx thought, his own philosophical tradition, this means that the labour of the human race had usurped the role of God: to be the subject of mediation and of reconciliation, in ultimate terms. Marx had observed this conclusion and spelt it out in terms of atheism: 'Once the essential reality of man in nature, man as the existence of nature for man, and nature for man as the existence of man, has become evident in practical life and sense experience, then the question of an alien being, of a being above nature and man—a question that implies an admission of the unreality of nature and man—has become impossible in practice'.[5] Labour makes God superflous; it solves the mystery of world history, it 'redeems' man and nature, becomes the instrument—and subject—of salvation in the universe of man. The ideological (and political) consequences of these statements will concern us further.

Marxist thoughts on the subject of labour have also

50

other levels. Work is not only seen in terms of these eschatological and cosmic concepts. It is also analyzed in terms of a fundamentally human and social phenomenon in the world of men; it is 'the confirmation of man as a conscious species-being'.[6] In his labour is contained the specifically human world, a world which is different from that of other beings. As a working being, producing in a human way, man is different from the other creatures. Of course, the animals also produce. But they produce only for their immediate needs. They produce one-sidedly and in one dimension, whereas man produced universally and in the round. He produces, not only out of physical necessity, but out of freedom. 'Man also fashions things according to the laws of beauty'.[7] This work, the freely creative and beautiful activity of man, is distinctively human, our own characteristic, the true being of man.

The clear recognition of the dignity of human labour is not the whole of the Marxist philosophy of work. This is the major theme, but to it there must be added in counterpoint the other theme of the young Karl Marx: the analysis of the real situation and the conditions of his contemporaries in the working process. It is not only the mature, but already the young Karl Marx who resists the abstract anthropology which ignores the actual living conditions of his fellow men. In these conditions, labour looks very different from the theory of free, creative, beautiful activity. Here work is seen as compulsion and poverty, weariness and deprivation, as a reducing and a threat to humanity. Expressed in a central concept as 'work is alienation'.

What does Marx understand by this important concept? He fastens upon a rich tradition of theological and philosophical thought, particularly in the thinking of Hegel and Feuerbach. The formal explanations given by Feuerbach are of particular importance: self-alienation consists of the temptation of (religious) man

51

to project his wishes and longings on to an imaginary concept, namely God. This means wishful thinking and uprooting himself from his world and his time. The creator himself, man, will then be sacrificed to his own creation, his own idea. One may then speak of a 'fetish' tendency.

Marx makes good use of this 'fetish' component in his analysis of alienation. But unlike Feuerbach, he goes far beyond the idea of religious consciousness. For him, the real location of alienation is not in religion, but in social economics.

His approach leads to the following: 'The object that labour produces, its product, confronts it as an alien being, as a power independent of the producer'.[8] In his original, not yet alienated, work man created for his need and for his joy. He related himself to the objects of his creation in a direct and personal way. They were products of his free and creative activity and therefore his relation to them was free. So far, there is no trace of fetishism. The world of objects is for man, not yet a strange, threatening, or ultimately hostile power.

It was only in the course of history that this alienated work arose. And it arose just at the point where a class society was formed, when the division of the social production process among different groups led to one group gaining possession of the means of production. Then the labourer worked and produced, but the product of his labour did not belong to him. It belonged to the possessor of the means of production and finally to the real controller of the whole work process, the power of money, to capital. Capital itself is the outcome of the work process, and therefore also a creation of the workers. In the name of the ruling economic system an unhealthy change has taken place in the original relation between 'subject' and 'object' or to express it in theological terms, which Marx did not use, but which I think makes his accusation much clearer, between

'Creator' and 'Creation'. Just as in Romans 1, Paul sees the typical strategy of sin in the great reversal of the roles of Creator and creature, and thus rooted in idolatory; so similarily in Marx, human alienation is rooted in the capitalist fetishism. Marx categorizes the devil's circle of this fetishism very impressively: 'The worker produces him, he then, man himself, as worker, as produce of his work, is the product of the whole process'.[9]

At the beginning of this unholy process stands the economic fact of the division of labour. There is nothing demonic in this. The necessity for division of labour arises in the organizing of every society—even the smallest which is the family. But when these normal procedures are enforced under the terms of a class society, the cloven hoof begins to appear; 'With the division of labour . . . comes at the same time the division—and that means unequal division, quantitatively and qualitatively—of labour and the products of labour'.[10] Groups and individuals arise, some of whom have more and some of whom have less. Private property arises and with it conflict between individuals and human groups. One further destructive decline comes. In the process of division of labour, whole sections of society are forced into one particular kind of work, they are assigned roles, an activity is given to each of them. These tendencies lead to the weakening and finally the destruction of freedom, creativity and joy in human work—such losses are aspects of alienation.

These things happened very quickly in the class society. their high point was reached in the alienation of the capitalist system. There, the tendencies outlined were taken to their logical conclusion. The social process fell ever more sharply into its elements—capital and labour. Antagonisms arose which for the weaker partner, i.e. the worker, were fatal. 'Labour produces

53

works of wonder for the rich, but nakedness for the worker. It produces palaces, but only hovels for the worker; it produces beauty, but cripples the worker; it replaces labour by machines but throws a part of the workers back to a barbaric labour and turns the other part into machines. It produces a culture, but also imbecility and cretinism for the worker'.[11]

Make no mistake: these smart words of Marx are not the words of a moralist. Already in the young Marx we can trace the outline of his later theory of economics. The emphases are already there. The alienating tendencies of the economic system are no accidents, no morally regrettable incidents, no lapse from good conduct. The real problem lies in the system itself. Alienation is the inevitable consequence of the system, an 'economic logic' is working itself out. Again and again, Marx seeks to illustrate and formulate this truth. His neatest formula is: 'The depreciation of the human world takes place in direct proportion to the increase in value of the world of things'.[12]

It is worthwhile reflecting on these statements of Marx's theory of alienation. He indicates two aspects of the theory, which from my understanding seem to characterize the whole Marxist theory and practice, also in its later form. On the one hand, the expression of a radically humanist assessment. Marx protests hence, also, against the suppression of the creative subject, man, by the power of the object: against the reduction of human existence to the level of things. In this he stands in the best tradition of Christian humanism. It is in this tradition that Immanuel Kant formulated his 'categorical imperative' for humanity with the sentence that man must never be treated simply as a means to an end. This clear statement of the humanist tradition can be traced in the background of Marx's analysis of alienation. In concrete economic terms, he states the legitimate relation between man and object, between labour and capital. The fetishism of the world of labour which Marx condemns is an expression of the basic form of inhumanity—and is attacked as such.

Side by side with this humanistic philosophy which is at the heart of his theory, the analysis of the young Karl Marx has another element—a scientific theory. Unlike the moralists, he seeks to construct and formulate the 'laws of national economy'. One can understand why Marx was anxious to do this, although he does not develop it fully until later. Marx struggled all his life to get free from moral solutions to social problems. This was an important concern which the Christian churches as well as theologians would do well to heed. There is no denying that this side of Marxism also has its dangerous tendencies: the temptation to describe the world of man in terms of discovered laws and to manipulate in a doctrinaire fashion. This tendency grew ever stronger in the development of Marxism: it certainly reached its climax (after Engels's attempt to show that Marxism could be a science of nature) in dogmatic Stalinism, in his argument that the *Universe—Earth—Man* (the title of a school textbook, also used in Germany) is explained out of an infallible theory. In the face of these temptations to dogmatic Marxism, we see the importance of the encounter with the young Karl Marx in the Christian-Marxist dialogue. The need is clearly there to return again and again to the humanistic basis of Marxist philosophy. In this way we can be reminded of the presence of that other tendency in the original Marxism and reflect critically upon its strengths and its dangers.

The Phenomenology of Alienation

In this survey we have so far only worked over the basic form of the Marxist view of alienation. On this basic structure other kinds of alienation develop until

55

they infect all levels of human existence. The greater part of the Paris manuscripts, and also the other early texts of Karl Marx, as well as the later works, including *Das Kapital,* is given over to a keen analysis of this dehumanizing phenomenon. Under its name one could describe the manifold reduction of the humanity of man. Under the lordship of capital, the worker is reduced to a product. All must be ruled by the heartless law of the market—even the production of man. 'If the production is much greater than the demand, then part of the labour force must be allowed to fall into the state of beggars or even die of hunger . . . The worker has become a product, and it is lucky for him if he can manage to become a man'.[13]

This 'luck' is highly questionable. Not only because in the early forms of capitalism, which Marx knew, the working man was unlikely to rise above the subsistence level, nor be able to satisfy more than his simplest 'animal' needs. But far more because of the nature of the work itself. Man was deprived of this deepest creative opportunity to become human by his work. He was degraded to the level of struggling simply to live. His work was not free labour, but oppressive forced labour. It is not the satisfaction of a need, but only the means to deal with the need without satisfying it'.[14] Because, according to Marx, as we have seen, work is the setting for a true humanity, alienated labour strikes at the root of meaningful life. The very nature of man is perverted: 'Life becomes simply a means for existence'.[15]

It is not only man as an individual who is destroyed, but man as a social being also, the human relations of fellowship and community. It is part of Marx's anthropological realism that he always regards man as *homo socialis,* a social being. He is never an isolated individual, but lives his personal life as man in relation to others. 'When man faces himself, he faces the other

56

man'.[16] Alienation has a social dimension. A perverted system of production necessarily produces perverted human relations.

That is shown by the fact that in the world of alienated labour it is the character of human relations which is most deeply affected. This can be seen at once in the relationship between representatives of the two opposing classes, labour and management. A developed industrial society is especially threatened with this. In earlier periods, personal relationships were still possible across the hierarchical divide. Even in the unjust system of feudalism it was possible to sustain personal relationships between master and servant, craftsman and apprentice, lord and serf, within a recognized system. It is quite different in a society structured by capitalism. With its dehumanized, fetish-based profit attitude, human factors are excluded from its impersonal, technocratic and economic system. For the capitalist, the worker means power. For the worker, the manager appears, in so far as he is personally known at all, as an exponent of an alien, exploiting power.

This interpersonal alienation must not be misunderstood as a moral issue. It has nothing to do with 'evil intent' on either side—and so this reason it cannot be solved by 'good intentions'. It results from the changed nature of the alienated world. The heaviest weight of this change falls naturally upon those who are caught in the wheels of this 'system'—namely, the workers. Yet, the young Karl Marx makes quite clear that all who take part in this alienation ultimately suffer.

In a world where humanity has become so reduced, human qualities themselves die, because men profit first economically and then socially from the misery of their fellow men. Even the capitalists, despite all their power and authority, are ultimately only slaves of this alienated world of labour. However, one must not overlook the difference in the weight of suffering.

57

'When worker and capitalist suffer, the worker suffers in his very existence, while the capitalist suffers in profits of his dead mammon'.[17] Yet, they suffer together: the human nature of the lords of production is also alienated by the lordly nature of their relationships; they too, whether they know it or not, lose their human face. It is here that the totality and universality of alienation becomes most clear. In such a world, no one wins. In so far as the humanity of man is the goal of human history, all lose. Human nature makes no decisive or important advance.

Who then triumphs in this alienated world? Who is the real master of this vicious circle? Karl Marx suggests at the end of his analysis in the Paris manuscripts the following answer: 'Private property is the product, result and necessary consequence of externalized labour'.[18] Here then is named the name of the real 'harvest' of the dehumanized system of production. It is not a god. It is not nature. It is not a man. It is a fetish: private property, mammon, capital. We must now follow Karl Marx and discuss this real winner, this idol of the alienated world.

The Diabolical Power of Money

When Karl Marx had reached the summit of his achievements and outlined his criticism of the economic system in heavy, regrettably unfinished, volumes of his life work, he called it *Das Kapital*. Behind that title lay the conviction that it was precisely this power which was the real source of the economic and political and human misery of millions of his contemporaries. He was convinced that a real criticism of political economy and corresponding political action must be launched on this front. This diagnosis does not only belong to his later period. Already in the *Economic and Philosophical Manuscripts* of the Paris period—and in other early writings—he rises with determined and passionate deliberation to the theme: Money.

Money appears in the analysis of the young Karl Marx as the quintessence of the alienated world. The whole process of alienation is concerned ultimately with this object: 'Money, since it has the property to appropriate all objects to itself, is thus the object *par excellence*. It is the universal character of this property which creates the omnipotence of money'.[19] The word 'omnipotent' is not to be taken as an exaggeration, but literally. 'Omnipotent' is the correct description to use for this subject. Marx does not hesitate to mobilize the language of the poet, the terminology of the theologian, and the style of mythology to express his understanding of this matter: 'Power', 'Divinity', 'God', 'Omnipotent' are appropriate concepts to use in the context of the problem of money.

Wherein lies the omnipotence of money? First, quite simply in that money possesses real power. Marx recalls Goethe, or rather Mephistopheles in *Faust:*

> Six stallions, say, I can afford,
> Is not their strength my property?
> I tear along, a sporting lord,
> As if their legs belonged to me.

That means: 'What I have thanks to money, what I pay for, i.e. what money can buy, that is what I, the possessor of money, am myself. My power is as great as the power of money. The properties of money are my—its owner's—properties and faculties'.[20] The range of human possibilities in no way depends upon personal qualifications. On the contrary, they play a secondary role. If I have wonderful personal abilities, but no money, these abilities do not help me very much. On the other hand, if I have no great ability, but money, I am, despite all, 'qualified'.

This omnipotence of money is treated dialectically by Marx. It is both 'divine' and 'diabolic'. It is divine.

Is this not an attribute of God in our western tradition, that he should be 'omnipotent'? Is it not his nature and also his function to work miracles, so that he is eternally exercising his power, and finally that he can make total changes, such as for example in the doctrine of *creatio ex nihilo* (creation out of nothing). That is a very good analogy to the function of capital. This is expected of money: it changes all things, it creates something out of nothing. Marx illustrates this divine likeness of the omnipotence of money: 'I am ugly, but I can buy myself the most beautiful woman. Consequently I am not ugly, for the effect of ugliness, its power of repulsion, is annulled by money . . . I may have no intellect, but money is the true mind of all things and so how should its possessor have no intellect?'.[21]

This 'divine' omnipotence of money is also at the same time diabolic, or as Marx prefers to express it, 'whorish'. Shakespeare, whom Marx loves to quote, has rightly said, in *Timon of Athens,* that money is not only visible divinity, but also seen to be the 'common whore of mankind'. Wherein lies the omnipotence of money? In its power to buy anything. But the concept, 'to be able to buy anything' is the concept of the prostitute, the universal prostitute. The most character-istic quality of money, namely to barter and exchange everything, shows it to be the matchmaker of men and races. It is the universal inverter of human values. It can 'change fidelity into infidelity, love into hate, hate into love, virtue into vice, vice into virtue, slave into master, master into slave, stupidity into intelligence and intelligence into stupidity'.[22] Money makes possible 'the fraternization of incompatibles' and forces 'opponents to embrace'.[23] This capacity to invert, confuse and exchange all human qualities is in a real sense diabolic and perverting.

It is clear that under the rule of money that which is

truly human will suffer. In the world of mammon there is no room for personal, compassionate love of neighbour. Here there is only room for the play of economic forces and here man becomes the football of alienated economic interests, an offering to the economic hunter.

The original sense of human production is fundamentally altered. The natural aim of economy is to satisfy human need: man is thus the aim of production. Under the rule of money all this changed. The purpose of economic activity now becomes, not to satisfy needs, but to create them. Marx illustrates this strategy very clearly: 'Each man considers how he can create new needs in his neighbour, force him to make a new sacrifice, place him in a new state of dependence and lead him into a new style of pleasure and with this bring him to economic ruin'.[24] No method is shunned. 'No eunuch flatters his oppressive master more, nor seeks to entice him into the gratification of new appetites more seductively to his own profit, than does the industrial eunuch, the producer, entice the golden bird, surreptitiously sneaking the widow's mite from the pocket of his dear Christian neighbour. Every product is a bait, with which the other is caught and his money lured away from him; each need, real or imaginary, is a weakness which leads the bird into the trap'.[25]

This dehumanizing tendency does not stop at the capitalists. The image that has already been used of 'industrial eunuchs', the producers, makes this quite clear. The real hero of this industrial world is not the rich man who lives luxuriously—that is a typical figure of the period of feudalism—but a neat, prosaic, well-mannered manager. His slogan is 'The less you eat, drink, spend on books, go to the theatre, to the dance, to the club, think, love, philosophize, sing, paint, write poetry, the more you will save, the greater will be your

61

treasure, which neither moth nor rust will corrupt, your capital'.[26] The extravagant individual would soon be swallowed up by the capitalist system, which lives by the rule, 'The less you are, the more you have'.[27]

In this fundamental law the real point of a world alienated by money is clearly expressed. It is a fatal denial and perversion of human reality. The category of 'having' strangles the category of 'being'. A formula which encapsulates the total perversion of the basic value of man. The categorical imperative of humanity (which we have already quoted from Kant) is thus destroyed by a frontal attack. Man has become the means of economic achievement; the true subject of production has become an object, a thing. Yet the capitalist has never once reached the goal of his economic activity: he too is destroyed by the power of money. The dehumanizing of the alienated world is complete.

Becoming Totally Human

Marx was not content in his early writings to analyze the alienated world and then name the root of its alienation. In his work on the nature of man, he described the phenomenology of alienation, not as a detached observer, but as a revolutionary thinker, intending to find a way out of the devil's circle and away from an inhuman system. As we read Marx, therefore, we very soon meet the question of how it is possible to overcome human alienation. His answer comes only in suggestions. Always he believes that it can be overcome. He puts forward his own suggestions in the form of an illustration and a programme: the sketch of a communist society. Marx does not approve of all that has been described under the title 'communism' in the course of history. A 'crude communism'—taken in a literal and unimaginative sense—is not real progress. For example, such a communism would change the traditional marriage for a common use of women. In the same way 'negative communism', which either denies all bourgeois values or makes all values alike, is a very dubious achievement. A real solution comes only with 'positive communism'.

Marx expects much, indeed all, from this positive communism. He sees this positive communism 'as the positive abolition of private properety which is human self-alienation and therefore the real re-appropriation of the human essence by and for man. This is the complete and conscious return of man conserving all the riches of previous development for man himself as a social, i.e. a human being'.[28] In these words the wide horizon of communism as understood by Marx is most clearly and unequivocally expressed. In the communist society we are concerned not with some new step in the social and historical development of man, but with a radical leap forward, which is qualitatively new in world history. With it the 'Babylonian captivity' of alienation is smashed and overcome. The great Exodus out of the 'kingdom of necessity' into the 'kingdom of freedom' has taken place, the new redeemed world has arrived.

The beginnings of this new world are simple and clear to describe: they are measured by the overcoming of private property. This, according to Marx, corresponds to the logic of history as the various levels of alienation arose because of the coming of private property, so the process of redemption is by way of the abolition of private property. With the fall of this 'evil enemy', the way lies open for the creation of total freedom for man. This is not only on the economic field but in every important human activity. We shall try to sketch the outline and consequences of this 'total humanizing' as understood by Marx.

With the overcoming of private property we reach the basic form of alienation: the relation of man to the economic product, the world of objects. The unholy fetishism by which man is alienated from the product of his work and he himself becomes degraded to a slave of his own creation, capital, will be totally destroyed in a communist system. The fruit of the working process goes, undiminished, to the working man; it remains his product and not that of an alien power. So the worker in his work remains himself. He remains from beginning to end of his operation what he really is: the free subject of his own economic and political history, the free creator of his own product.

That has profound consequences for our relation to the world of objects. 'Private property has made us so stupid and short-sighted that an object is only ours when we have it, when it exists as capital for us or when we directly possess, eat, drink, wear, inhabit it, in short when we use it . . . Thus all physical and spiritual senses have been replaced, by the simple alienation of all these senses, by the sense of having'.[29] In the revolutionary breakthrough we recognize that this stupid strategy of having shuts us off from the world of objects with its rich variety and naturalness. Marx speaks expressly in this connection of the renewal of the senses, of the 'complete emancipation of all human senses and qualities'.[30] Whereas a merchant, or an observer who thinks like a merchant, sees only the market value of a mineral or a work of art, one who has been set free from fetishism sees the beauty of the object and its rich variety.

The destruction of the power of private property— the power of capital—makes possible the humanizing of the working process. The clear direction in which this leads is not developed in the Paris documents, but somewhat later in the *German Ideology* (which Marx wrote with Engels). Here it is expected that the communist societyt will overcome all the one-sidedness of work which has been forced upon the worker in his earlier role—and that meant for his whole life. Things will be quite different in a communist society. Then the working process would be associated freely with the worker and no one would be bound to any one exclusive field of work. The possibility would be open to all citizens 'to do this today, that tomorrow; to hunt in the morning; afternoon to fish; evening to look after the cattle; after eating, to criticise, as I wish; without becoming a hunter, or a shepherd or a critic'.[31]

These ideals are a bit romantic and to this day in Marxist, Communist States still utopian. The rigidity of social activity has not always softened, but rather in centralized, planned economies, it has sometimes hardened. Yet, the Marxist indication is not without importance, perehaps not as a 'law', but as 'gospel', which means an indication of the desired direction in which society should develop. Work should become what it was in its original human function: a free, creative, spontaneous unfolding of human competence and potential.

The overcoming of alienation in the revolutionary abolition of private property also heals the wound of separation in inter-personal relations. The communist society makes the original dream of a human fellowship come true. The economic antagonism, which in a class society tears apart the social organization and under the rule of capital endangers and destroys personal relations between fellow men, is done away with when private property is abolished. But other antagonisms also disappear. Marx includes here, the cultural alienation of religions and ideologies (this means also the opposition between materialism and idealism); political alienation in the state; the alienation of the nuclear family. The communist man turns away from these perversions and restrictions back to his human i.e. social, being. Marx could already see on the horizon of the new society, new and truly human relationships.

And not only on the horizon! In this present situation, Marx declared that the opportunity for a new humanity was in no way a future dream. It can be seen already in the still alienated field of labour. In one of the most personal parts of his manuscript Marx tells of a moving experience with the Paris workers:

> When the communist workers come together, it is first of all for teaching, propaganda, etc. But at the same time there is evident a natural need, a need for company, and so the means becomes the purpose. This practical movement can be seen in its most brilliant form by observing the French *ouvriers* together. Smoking, drinking, eating, etc., are no longer means for bringing them together, or social methods. The company, the coming together, the entertainment, which again has fellowship for its purpose, takes them over. The brotherhood of man is no mere slogan, but the truth with them. The jewel of humanity shines upon us as we see these forms, hardened by work, coming together'.[32]

In the community of freely associated working activity; in a situation of fellowship, in which no one is a means used for an economic, political or egotistical end, but discovers his life in true brotherhood as the purpose, then human alienation will be overcome. The riddle of history will be solved in communism.

Questions

The Marxist image of man poses a serious question for Christian theology. How are we to take up this question? We shall attempt this in three ways:

1. First I would like to deal with the humanist attack and the concrete contribution of Marxist anthropology. The idea of humanity belongs to the classical emphasis of the European tradition. Already

in the time of Marx many of his contemporaries were turning towards this central position. Yet, it appears to me that there were very few thinkers to whom the title 'humanist' could be more readily applied in that period of neo-humanism than to the young Karl Marx. With him 'humanist' meant more than 'the idea of humanity', but a passionate desire for the concrete relationships and living conditions which defined humanity. His philosophy had glimpsed with high realism the everyday distress of the people in his day, and had set out to analyze and deal practically with the situation.

Two aspects of this programme appear to me to be of special relevance, particularly for Christian theology. Marx widened and deepened the anthropological debate, placing new emphasis upon the dimensions of history, of society and of labour and setting them firmly in the foreground. Of course, these three emphases did not amount to a 'discovery': they could be found in previous histories of philosophy and theology. In particular, they were to be found in biblical teaching: the stress on the social and historical character of man, the high value given to work (as distinct from that in classical thinking) is clearly central to biblical anthropology. In practice these three dimensions of man are seen to be valid for an image of man.

Despite this it must be said that in the general stream of anthropological tradition this aspect of the study of man has been neglected. The idealistic understanding of man has been widely emphasized and with it quite other views of the nature of man. How often has man been described as of timeless nature, as though he were isolated, or as understood with detached academic concern. One has only to think of the philosophies of ancient Greece and their influence upon the Christian humanist tradition. Idealist anthropology brought with it many important insights for humanism, but they have given a one-sided and restricted view of human reality. Marxist 'historical materialism' has brought out into the full light the 'under-exposed' dimensions and set in motion not only anthropology, but the whole world of man itself.

In this way, Marx has clarified the classical humanist outlines in a truly human form. We have already shown what role the 'categorical imperative' of humanity has played in the background of his analysis of alienation. He has passionately protested against the 'thingness' of man, wherever it has been stressed, and against every sacrifice of the human subject to the impersonal forces of the objective world. Alienation means for him the loss of man as the subject. Man can defeat alienation by the power of man, becoming the subject of his own destiny. Unlike most other humanists, Marx does not consider that the problem to be solved is primarily idealistic or ethical—somewhat in the sense of the integrity of the moral idea—rather a problem, questioning the economic and social conditions of alienation.

I find this dialectical relationship of the classical humanist view, with the appeal for its concrete expression in political economy, the real and abiding contribution of the young Karl Marx to the history of European humanism. It is also clear that this work, particularly in its dialectic, has fruitful possibilities for a meeting between Christians and Marxists. The young Marx poses critical questions for both sides. For the Christians he has posed the question as to whether, in the actual history of Christianity, they have sufficiently seriously taken up the issues of alienation. For the Marxists he has posed the question whether they in the course of their history have taken into account sufficiently the humanists' criticism of their basic theory and practice. Although we have no intention of playing off the young Karl Marx against the 'old', there seems little doubt that we must turn to the young Karl Marx if we are to get to the heart of the Christian-Marxist dialogue.

2. Another aspect of the anthropoligical outline written by the young Karl Marx has particular importance for the meeting between Christians and Marxists: the presence in it of strong biblical motives and insights, and its closeness to the biblical heritage. Of course, the young Karl Marx is already a declared atheist. Of course, he has already separated himself form theology and the church. And yet there are traces of biblical ways of thinking in his thought which have not been recognized—these are not simply vestiges, but they are pointers. This fact is particularly important for the Christians to recognize. It should prevent them from condemning the work of Marx as simply his atheism or his materialism. Such a condemnation could be refuted or at least blunted in the light of real echoes of the biblical message.

I will select a few examples of biblical themes and motivation in Marx. We may look at once at the key concept of 'alienation'. We have already shown his direct philosophical heritage in Hegel and Feuerbach and we shall not attempt to minimize that. But it raises a question; does this concept not have its setting in a much older Judaeo-Christian way of thinking? Is he not really borrowing from the concept of redemption history, which describes the human situation as between the 'Fall' and 'Salvation', as we find it in the Bible? Can we recall the basic law of alienation as Marx describes it, the structure of his argument about the strategy of 'fetishism', without remembering the way in which the Bible characterizes the strategy of sin? Perhaps the most telling parallel of all is in the biblical explanation of the grounds of alienation—seen in idolatry—when men exchanged the creator for the creature (Romans 1:18-32). *Mutatis mutande,* this is what the Marxist says about the analysis of alienation: the process by which the worker, the true creator, is changed into the product, the thing he created, by capital. This is the fundamental alienation.

More important than the structural similarities is the concrete substance of the way the Marxist develops his arguments. Here too we come across a parallel to biblical ways of thinking. Think of his treatment of the power of capital over the worker and its dehumanizing consequences for human life. Doesn't his exposition of the hostile role of money bear a remarkable resemblance to what the Bible says about the enslaving power of Mammon? The way in which Marx characterizes the rule of capital often with the concept of 'the powers', expresses something akin to the biblical witness against the dark rule of the demonic 'principalities and powers' who seek to lay hold of mankind, enslaved by sin.

Above all it is in the statement that the original power of alienation lies in the power of Mammon that the relation to the biblical perspective becomes clearest. That the power of money can corrupt and alienate man in a peculiarly dangerous way is clearly biblical. It's no accident that in the well-known words of Jesus, Mammon is styled a kind of anti-God. His words are formulated as a statement of alternative choice: 'No one can serve two masters . . . You cannot serve God and Mammon' (Matthew 6:24). And the apostle sees the basic situation of alienation in the same way. One thinks of the words: 'The love of money is the root of all evil' (I Timothy 6:10). Here the love of money is directly described as the radical evil—and its consequences very clearly pictured: 'It is through this craving that some have wandered away from the faith and pierced their hearts with many pangs'.

We are not dealing here with passing references, but with the whole direction and thrust of the biblical message. it is already clear in the Old Testament prophets and culminates in the message of Jesus. It consequently takes the side of the poor and the oppressed, and denounces the unrighteous Mammon. Fritz Lieb, who was one of the first of the theologians to busy himself with the young Karl Marx, was right when he maintained in the light of this influence of the biblical message, 'despite his show of being an atheist, Marx very strongly developed the high points of his doctrine from his knowledge of the Gospel'.[33] One must also agree with Fritz Lieb when he continues 'It is a kind of pious godlessness when, from the Christian side, one minimizes the weight of his opponent's argument because he is not avowedly "Christian"'.[34] Even from a biblical and theological point of view, Karl Marx's analysis of alienation must be taken seriously.

3.   While we are taking the Marxist question to the church and theology seriously, we must not allow ourselves to forget the serious questions posed by theology to the Marxist anthropology. Apart from the similarities, there are also differences between the Marxist and the Christian image of man. I am not only thinking of the atheistic elements in the Marxist view. This is naturally a central issue with which we shall have to deal. At this point, I want simply to question two themes which are central to the Marxist view and which need questioning critically from a theological point of view. They are two central themes of Marxist anthropology and are closely related to each other: his concepts of alienation and of labour.

My first question concerns the restricted alienation theory which Marx limits to economics. That Marx spent his life on the decisive importance of economics for the quality of human life is without doubt his major contribution in his anthropology. This strength becomes a problem. All other fields are subordinated to it, all problems seen from the economic point of view. This does not happen crudely or without refined analysis in Marx's work. His later theory of the economic foundation with the cultural superstructure must not be misunderstood as mechanistic or monolithic. Yet, it can hardly be denied that this is the tendency with all Marxist thinkers. Not only in the Marx of his later years, nor first by Engels, Lenin or Stalin, but even in the young Karl Marx, there is already a tendency towards an over-valuing of the economic dimension in the study of man. His alienation theory shows this. The 'root of all evil' lies in the economic relationship, to be precise, in private property. And on the positive side, it is the revolution in relation to private property that sets the healing process in motion.

I take this doctrinaire statement of Marxist alienation to be an anthropological restriction, a simplification of the complexity of relationships in the world of alienated man. It has very serious consequences. The 'localizing' of evil in one arouses the expectation that a revolutionary change in this area—the radical socialization of the means of production—would lead to the overcoming of alienation in general. That is a dangerous illusion. It leads to underestimating the power of evil in the new society. For example, in a socialist society, new, highly dehumanizing forms of alienation can arise which are insufficiently considered and politically suppressed. This can happen in the political, cultural and spiritual field. There are many examples in socialist states, particularly those dogmatically governed, to show evidence of this tendency. It is my opinion that this is closely connected with the economically restricted anthropology of the Marxists.

In this connection, the Christian concept of sin would greatly clarify the situation. This is admittedly a misunderstood and suspect concept. But when it is biblically understood it expresses the radical nature and complex strategy of evil. Alienation as sin is no marginal comment. It cannot be once and for all localized in one area nor fixed at one stage of development. It has to do with the heart of human reality, submerging all levels of personal and social development. It has to do with the sober truth. Not in the sense of defeatism or fatalistic resignation when faced with evil. The church's teaching about sin would be unbiblical if it reduced men to helplessness. In the biblical context, the 'Fall' is seen as part of the dynamic history of salvation. Man plays his part and does not capitulate before the concrete forms of alienation. The meaningfully new is possible in history and is necessary. But, the last victory over alienation transcends the possibilities of history, as the kingdom of God. It is well not to forget this, in the concrete situation of humanity.

My second question is connected with this. It concerns the Marxist concept of work or labour. That Karl Marx, in his thinking, has developed the many-sided character, and understood the importance, of work from the point of view of understanding man is a fact of significance also for theology. Christian social ethics has much to learn from the Marxist philosophy of work. The Marxist view of humanity with its world-changing activity is a real challenge to the Christian understanding of man. It is not the value of labour which is the point at issue between Marxist and Christian, but rather the place of labour in the world of man. What kind of a function does labour have in the context of human history?—this is one of the decisive questions in the Marxist-Christian dialogue. Karl Marx, as we have seen already in the young Karl Marx, places the importance of labour at the end of the process in a sense of giving it meaning: the free labour of the revolutionary man is not simply placed under the promise of a radical, albeit relative, change in the world, but is seen as the universal cure in a cosmic setting. The ontological gap between nature and history, matter and spirit, subject and object is bridged by the creative activity of generations of men, the knot of world history is undone.

From the biblical and theological point of view, so high a value placed upon the historical work of man will not do. The history of production is a clearly defined part of world history. It is no 'redemption' history. Work is the right, but not the justification of man. Paul's protest in the New Testament against justification by works—mobilized at the Reformation against the medieval 'earned piety'—has its reality also in the meeting with Marxists. It is the undoubted duty of theology to bear witness to this central assertion of the Gospel message in a capitalist as well as in a socialist society and to make it credible and clear. It does not so much bring its inherited doctrine to man, but resists every tendency towards a faithless humanity. Every justification by works means being able to overcome without grace and has its consequence ultimately in a loss of grace. In its claim to hold the key to the riddle of history, by its own strength to bring about the final solution, it tends to the absolutizing of its position, to harden the lines—particularly when it has power in its own hands—and to make a fetish of its achievements. It is not in this way the alienation in the world of men will be overcome, because a humanity without grace creates new alienations.

It seems to me, that on this point the temptation of Marxist thinkers can be diagnosed in his history of activity theologically and anthropologically. The Marxists are not the only ones to whom this can happen. In the capitalist understanding of man, the temptation to justification by works is no less. Karl Marx has pointed out more sharply than any other philosopher the graceless consequences of capitalism—for example

74

in its triumph of 'having' over 'being'. He has not so critically reflected upon his own conscious theories without grace. The graceless consequences of Marxism have meanwhile become clearer. There are Marxists who have already worked critically on this. And in this the problem of Marxist atheism has come again into the forefront. There are good reasons. The Marxist question about man also remains inseparably bound up with the question of God.

3. The Challenge of Marxist Criticism of Religion:

Atheism out of the Spirit of the Age

'As far as Germany is concerned, the criticism of religion is essentially complete, and the criticism of religion is the presupposition of all criticism'. With this opening sentence of his famous essay, *Towards a Critique of Hegel's Philosophy of Right,* Karl Marx's historic standpoint in his criticism of religion was clearly determined.[35] Marx fastened on to the rich heritage of the German criticism of religion and followed it closely through to its logical conclusion with growing sympathy. Which heritage are we here concerned with?

The beginnings of Marxist thought are very closely bound up with the controversies surrounding the philosophical legacy of Hegel, as this was known in the cultural atmosphere of the 'forties last century. The early work which Marx undertook with Engels, *The German Ideology,* describes the situation clearly: 'In the general chaos, powerful kingdoms were formed, as soon to fall, heroes emerged briefly only to be flung into the darkness by more daring and more powerful rivals. It was a revolution, in the face of which the French Revolution was child's play, a world struggle, in comparison with which the struggles of the *diadochi* (Alexander's heirs) appeared trivial . . . In the three years 1842-45 more was cleared away in Germany than in three centuries before'.[36]

The conflict crystalized itself into two themes: Hegel's philosophy of right and of religion. Understandably, because here lay the social troubles of the day. On the one side, Germany experienced at this time an economic and a political impetus. On the other side, there developed in Prussia a strongly authoritarian regime, bureaucratic and military, with a strong police force, censorship and intrigue, against which many—especially the young German students— rebelled. This system had two authoritarian pillars: Throne and Altar. It went without saying that for the Prussian monarchy the ideal was 'The Christian State'. An upright piety closely bound up with Prussian 'rigour' was imprinted upon the bourgeois public image of the land.

In this context, Hegel's philosophy of religion and state was realized. Can the heritage of Hegel be claimed for the established order? This was the intention of most Hegelians who could be called 'orthodox'. From his Berlin chair, Hegel became the great author of the ideology for the system, the national, cultural interpreter and the expounder of the Prussian *Realpolitik*. There were some of his students, however, who asked if Hegel did not have another side to him. The great systematizer had also been the great dialectician. His philosophy was not only reconciliation with the given, but also the philosophy of the destruction of outworn forms. It was here that the burning question was stated: where does the true strength of this thinker lie? Which Hegel is the true and the real? Church and state recognized clearly the Hegel of the right wing. But ever louder came the voice of the other, revolutionary group of 'young Hegelians' declaring: 'The Hegel of the left is the right Hegel!' This group included men like Heinrich Heine, David Friedrich Strauss, Bruno Bauer, Ludwig Feuerbach, Max Stirner. They developed that tradition of German criticism which Marx also—though not uncritically—accepted.

It was typical of this group that they concentrated, sometimes exclusively, upon the criticism of religion. We shall try to sketch their position briefly.

The most important philosophical figure of this criticism of religion was without doubt Ludwig Feuerbach. He was brought up on theology and converted to philosophy by Hegel. For his whole life he retained an interest in religion, but he changed the signs. He concentrated upon one theme: religion, the irreconcilable struggle. Religion is in principle the lie, the radical evil in the world of men. In it man is alienated from himself. He is the creator, God is his idea, religious ideas and values are his projections. In religion, these facts become obscured and reversed. The religious man, the real creator, himself makes his creature, the God idea, into the authority who gives him orders, he loses his sovereignty. This self-alienation of man spreads its influence into every part of his life. The religious man becomes, by this sale of himself to his idol, alienated from his true origin in nature, alienated from other men and finally from himself. Thus religion proves itself to be the most evil form of misanthropy, which becomes most obvious in its tendency towards asceticism.

Man can be freed from this only by a radical rejection of religion. The alienating strategy of the religious disposition must be seen through, the lie must be unmasked by criticism of religion. Then the truth will become clear: theology is anthropology—God is the projection of man. Where this has been seen the way to human emancipation and enlightenment begins.

Beside this great radical of religious criticism, there stand lesser men, significantly many were theologians by profession. First the German theologian David Friedrich Strauss. With his book *The Life of Jesus,* he directed his attack against Hegel's attempts to reconcile philosophy and Christianity. By historical criticism of the New Testament he showed that the historical Jesus, which Strauss had set out to verify, did not exist. Christ is myth. god must be thought of as impersonal, the revelation of God is bound up, not with the history of Christ nor of the Christian, but with world history. In this sense, Hegel's philosophy of history carried to its logical conclusion meant the 'de-Christing' of history.

But for Marx the more important statements were those of the no less radical theologian of Bonn, Bruno Bauer. Bauer was trained as a New Testament scholar and at first in his controversy with Strauss was opposed to this extreme interpretation of Hegel. However, he soon changed to become a decisive critic of orthodox teaching. His main thesis was that the secret of the New Testament Gospel was the secret of the self-consciousness of the first Christians. The pious disposition of the biblical writer is the true subject of the Gospel.

In the development of this point of view Bauer came very close both to Hegel and to Strauss. Hegel had said that Christianity is in no way the highest form of the religious spirit; Strauss had said that Christianity has in no way a substance comparable with the divine. The human self-consciousness is all in all. With this conviction Bauer put all his energies into a bitter struggle against a theological interpretation of religion. The 'critical criticism' became his programme. He exercised in this way a powerful influence on the young Karl Marx, whose personal friend he became. Together they published a satirical book called *The Last Trump over Hegel, the Antichrist and Atheist.* But Marx did this very much against his will and therefore unfruitfully. He did not remain long with this attack of the 'critical criticism'. He separated himself from the 'holy family' of young Hegelians and even from his 'Saint Bruno'. He made his own way, starting from this position. For him too, the criticism of religion is complete—and the criticism of religion is the presupposition of all criticism.

What comes out of this brief survey of his cultural history for our understanding of Marx's criticism of religion? Only a provisional, but certainly not negligible, piece of information: Marx, as a critic of religion, thinks in conscious continuity with the criticism of his time. He lights upon the radical irreligious element in the cultural situation of his time and accepts it almost without question. The emphatic assurance of his critical friends that religion fundamentally endangers the emancipation of man and that the defeat of religion is essential for the liberation of man, has also for him an axiomatic validity.

One may occasionally debate with the Marxist scholars whether atheism is essential or merely accidental for Marxism. I do not find such activity very fruitful. The complexity of the question is not adequately dealt with by the discussion of abstract concepts. it is clear that the Marxist criticism of religion is a given factor of the situation of his time, and in that sense it is conditioned by the period in which he lived. No doubt this means that there is an 'accidental' element in it. This needs to be looked at by dogmatic Marxists who perpetuate the belief that their position is not a product of a period. Dogmatic Christians should also reflect upon the close relation between this criticism of the social conditions of the time. Such reflection must lead to self-criticism and the discovery of the Christian's own guilt in that the church in her relationships has provoked this radical criticism of religion.

With that we come to the second complex of our research:

The Critical Social Context

It would be a misunderstanding of Karl Marx's criticism of religion to think of it as hypotheses derived from the spirit of his time. It is in no way a 'reflex' of the cultural situation in which he lived. Of course, he shared the current assumptions about religion, but he developed the accepted religious criticism in a unique way, or better: he set it in the social and critical context of a radically new understanding of man and the world. This is formulated in his most important comments on the criticism of religion in his earlier writings, as for example in *Towards a Critique of Hegel's Philosophy of Right: Introduction* and *On the Jewish Question* (both Paris, 1844). It is clear from the beginning.

The position of the young Hegelians—particularly Feuerbach—is put forward as 'The foundation of irreligious criticism is this: man makes religion, religion does not make man'.[37] But this foundation is expressed quite differently and set in motion. Marx does this in the context of a thorough and detailed criticism of the thought of the young Hegelians, as this is expressed formally in the important *Theses on Feuerbach*. The human being is 'a collection of relationships' (Thesis 6), 'Man is none other than the world of man, the state, the society'.[38]

All this has important consequences for the interpretation of human alienation and for the value placed upon religion. We have seen in the previous chapter that the young Karl Marx took over the concept of alienation from Hegel and Feuerbach. But he treated it radically and concretely. Alienation does not originate, nor operate, in the restricted areas of the spiritual life, religion and speculative philosophy, but in the total world of men, particularly in their *ens realissimum,* in the social and economic spheres. Under the rule of private property, robbed of the product of his labour and emptied of any creative joy in his work, this working man's labour has become the root of universal perversion. What Feuerbach saw rooted in religious perversion—the oppression of man, who is the real creator, by God, who is really only man's creation—Marx saw in social and economic relationships. It is here that man is enslaved by his product and alienated on every side.

The first thing that emerges from this primary connection is that the religious form of alienation is secondary. The social and political relationships, i.e. state and society, 'produce religion, which is a perverted world consciousness, because they are a perverted world'.[39] It is in this actual context that the well-known words of Marxist criticism of religion have to be understood: 'The religious distress is in one, an expression of true distress, and in another the protest against that true distress.—Religion is the cry of the oppressed creature, the comfort of a heartless world, it is like the spirit of a spiritless condition. It is the opium of the people'.[40] You can see here a good example of the Marxist dialectic of the double motive— 'expression' and 'protest'. Marx differentiates. he does not lump them together, nor consider them in narrow 'linear' thinking, as the 'critical critics' have done before and after Marx. This popularizing of his criticism of religion in later Marxism is typified in the change of 'opium of the people' into 'opium for the people', thus turning religion into an instrument with evil intent to manipulate.

In this statement the Marxist criticism of religion is shown to be considerably different from that of his predecessors. For them, religion appears often as the quintessence of misanthropy. Their 'critical' or 'total' criticism was burdened with an anti-religious set of ideas. That is why they seem to be monotonously repetitive in their treatment of religion. This is quite foreign to Marx. Religion is not the root of all evil, the radical defect nor the sinful inheritance of mankind. Religion is not the reason for a perverted world, but a perverted world is the root of religion. One cannot make a 'scapegoat' out of religion. The criticism of religion is never to be pursued for its own sake as the major theme: 'The struggle against religion is part of the struggle against that world in which religion is the spiritual aroma'.[41] Criticism of religion is meaningful only in the setting of social criticism.

This statement has important consequences. Marx's relation to religion, in comparison with the religious criticism of his time, is much more actual. Religion must be understood predominantly in its concrete forms. It is important to establish which religious and ecclesiastical manifestations of religion are the target of Marx's attack. It is my assessment that his protest is mainly against two phenomena: the misuse of political power by Christendom and the worship of mammon in the religion of the time.

The first point appears in his notable, and to this day valid, criticism of the 'Christian states'. We have already noted the oppressive presence of this in the 'ideal' of the state philosophy and social climate of the Prussian monarchy. Marx suffered under this climate and protested against the ideology of the 'Christian state'. The alliance of throne and altar appeared to him an unholy misalliance. This was not a theological attack. His basis was social and political criticism. Yet, it is remarkable that in the context of a political argument he could so diagnose and sharply criticize the religious weaknesses in the idea of a Christian state. With clear reference to the biblical message, which the 'Christian state' should certainly have taken seriously, he described emphatically how 'the infamy of its secular aims, which religion covers with sanctity, and the glory of its religious consciousness, are in unresolved conflict'.[42] This he establishes in a way that should have come from the pen of a learned divine of the time.

But clearer and sharper comes the second basis of his polemic: the religious worship of mammon. We recall that money, mammon, capital is for Marx the highest power of the alienated world. It is also the highest God of religious alienation. Marx attempts to explain this in reference particularly to the Jewish religion: 'Money is the zealous God of Israel before whom no other God can stand'.[43] Usury is the 'secular worship' of the Jew. And not only the Jew. The God of the Jews has become the God of the world. The Jewish leaven has risen very quickly, especially in Christendom. But there is more. The Jewish spirit of mammon reaches its high point in the Christian bourgeois society. Marx recognizes the typical, 'pious' Christian of his time! Even the Gospel had become for many of them an article of trade. So Christianity which came from Judaism has once again been dissolved in Judaism. This is the cutting edge of Marx's criticism of religion.

In this socially critical dimension of Marxist atheism I see a continuing challenge to theology and the church. One cannot overlook the fact that this form of Christianity as political power and in the worship of mammon, has provoked this protest. And one must recognize without delay, that an attack on these two phenomena was and is just—both in its own terms and on theological grounds. The perversion of every politically established church can be shown from a biblical point of view. Such a church ignores the authentic teaching of Jesus, who urged the service of love rather than the love of mastery. Such a church betrays also his undoubted preference for the poor and the under-privileged. The worship of mammon is sharply and uncompromisingly denounced by the prophets and the apostles, and particularly by the challenging words of Jesus (Matthew 6:24). When Marx directs his criticism to this matter with such energy, he speaks, not simply from outside, but from within the radical tradition of the church. If we want to water down or silence this voice, perhaps with the excuse that it is a decidedly 'godless' voice, then we show signs that we are not ready for repentance. If the church evades the challenge of Karl Marx she may easily find herself evading the biblical challenge itself. Here to this day there is a chronic weakness among Christians.

A theology which is aware of the need for self-criticism will also, and must, pose critical questions to Marxist atheism, perhaps to Marx himself. Has he not in his careful differentiation and his important criticism of religion failed to take account of one point? While the criticism may be valid for the actual condition of the church, the question should be asked whether that condition is an 'accident' of the times, and whether Christianity in its true 'nature' is possible only in this condition and offers only this possibility? Marx appears to know that Christianity in its origin and also in its history offers other possibilities, but he does not take this into consideration in his theory of religion.

A similar and much further-reaching question must be posed to later Marxism. It is whether their theory of religion has not weakened the concrete, socially critical statement of Marx in favour of a general anti-religious theory into which it has been allowed to degenerate. Above all it is clear that wherever Marxism becomes the official ideology of a Marxist-Socialist State, it tends to freeze its atheistic standpoint, without reference to any actual existing form or changes in Christianity, into a general ideology—to the great loss of openness and dynamic in a socialist society, endangering co-operation in social work between Christians and Marxists.

These two questions lead us further into another, more general and more abstract (and to my mind more thoughtful) dimension of the Marxist criticism of religion. With this we come to the third part of our study.

The Dogmatic Anthropological Dimension of Marxist Atheism

Our historical treatment has already underlined the anthropological element in the background of the Marxist criticism of religion. The pseudo-secret of religion is the secret of human self-consciousness. Theology is in reality anthropology. Marx took up this thesis of the young Hegelians without hesitation: 'Man makes religion: religion does not make man'. He sharpened it. As we have shown in our treatment of the Critical Social Context, Marx filled out and made more concrete the theses of these young Hegelians. Here too he sharpened this thesis by rejecting every unhistorical and abstract anthropology. For him 'man' means 'the world of men'.

Now it is important to recognize that this valuable contribution of Marx which makes concrete the thinking about man, is not the last word. There is—especially in the context of criticism of religion—one further polemical point: Marx introduces the concept of the *aseitäs* of the world of man. *Aseitäs*—from Duns Scotus—is the concept of 'existence from itself' as distinct from 'existence dependent from another'. The *aseitäs* of the world of man establishes for Marx, with this thesis and in this context, atheism as a constituent part of his philosophy.

With the key word *aseitäs* (existence from itself) we are consciously using theological language. There is a distinct echo of the typical theological statement. Classical theology speaks of the *'aseitäs* of God', distinguishing the sovereign independence of the creator from the creation. Can we say then that by the very use of such a term the Marxist position is likely to be manipulated by theology from the beginning? I think not. Marx himself developed a perfectly adequate thesis on man and his world in the clear context of theology—especially in contradiction to the doctrine of creation.

I recall one of the key passages of his *Paris Manuscripts*. It is concerned with the central human problem of emancipation, the question of the true nature of man, understood not only speculatively, but in the deepest sense of man's practical and revolutionary protest. This eminently anthropological outline has an unmistakable element of religious criticism. Marx argues: 'A being is independent in so far as it stands on its own feet, and it first stands on its own feet when it has itself to thank for its existence. A man who lives by the grace of another carries himself as a dependent being. But I am totally dependent for life upon the grace of another, not only when I have to thank him for his support, but when in addition he has created my life . . . when it is not my own creation'.[44]

Marx is here clearly referring to the biblical teaching of God the creator and for him the nature of man is de-secularized by such a doctrine. The pre-condition of human freedom is that this God be abolished. If I understand him aright, until this is done I do not stand on my own feet and thus I have not been really emancipated—or to grasp the decisive, positive concept, I am not yet 'really' man. Therefore in the highest interest of the nature and freedom of man this God must be removed.

This is precisely what Marx attempts to do. With his 'left hand', without too much effort, he mobilizes a bit of negative criticism of religion, borrowing from the natural philosophy of his day, attacking the 'agruments for the existence of God' and the doctrine of creation. That is not his main thrust. In his main thrust he is positive and his attack upon religion is indirect. He develops a kind of socialist-communist doctrine of creation: 'In which . . . for the socialist man, the whole of so-called world history is none other than the produce of man by human labour, so that nature becomes for man, that he may have the visible, indisputable evidence of his birth. He arises by his own efforts'.[45]

Man bears the implications of this argument: the socialist-communist man—the fellowship of freely associated individuals, as Marx would later express it—carries the inheritance of the biblical creator God. Man is shown to be the true subject of the real and human history of creation and redemption. What in the biblical religion is solved only eschatologically in the kingdom of God, is now seen to be solved by man's 'objective activity', by his labour and revolution in history. In this way, all questions are answered, all relationships in the world of men are healed. The theological promise of 'reconciling all things' appears as the true restoration and real renewal 'of human nature, by and for man', the complete and conscious turning of man by and for himself to his social, i.e. human, nature. This conversion occurs within the development of the whole realm of man. And not only mankind—also in world history, yes even nature is fulfilled: 'This communism is the true resolution of the conflict between man and nature, between man and man, the true solution of the struggle between existence and being, between subjective and objective, between freedom and necessity, between individual and species. He is the solved riddle of history and knows himself as this solution'.[46]

According to my understanding, this dimension of the Marxist criticism of religion presents the second challenge and the real problem for Christian theology, and it does so in a positive as well as a loaded sense.

I would like to point out the positive side of this radical criticism of religion first. I am not thinking here only of its positive sense of purpose. This also is of value, that here we do not have atheism calling us to an empty nihilism, indifferent and tired of life as so often has happened in the history of atheism. Marx is concerned not with destruction but with building up not with disease but with healing. However the positive is not created by the mere description of this vision. What matters is not just the form, but above all the content. Marxist atheism thinks big: it is in no way blinkered by its own problems, nor isolated by generalizations, nor narrow-minded and sectarian in its treatment of religion as the real hydra of the sons of men which must be destroyed. We have often met this narrowness in bourgeois free thinking atheists. Not so Marxist atheism. Marxist atheism concentrates its thought, not chasing after arbitrary details, but deals with the central questions of the nature and freedom of man. It stands in the best tradition of European humanism—one might also say, Christian humanism! The Marxist criticism of religion is also unique in that it concerns itself with the central humanistic problems, but not as idealist or abstract. It attempts to study the 'reality' of man in the context of real social history. Hence it is concerned with setting in motion the social life of man towards freedom and hope. In all these emphases, the Marxist criticism of religion presents a challenge to theology.

It is for this reason that I hold the Marxist criticism

of religion—and also the whole Marxist theory with which it is bound up—to be the high point of European criticism of religion. A Christian theology does not accept this challenge, which wants to evade the hard points of this theory and which does not attempt to find common ground with the positive elements in these concerns, would demonstrate its own narrow-mindedness and blindness, rather than its sovereignty and objectivity.

The exclusive concentration of Marxist theory of religion upon the central issues—the 'reality' and emancipation of man—raises specific critical questions for Christian theology. Questions must also be raised about the actual form and consequences of the humanistic contours of Marxist criticism of religion. To be precise: Is there not a danger that, by this criticism, positions will become fixed and attitudes unyielding, so that sooner or later the main contours are endangered in theory and practice? As I see it, it is just here that Marxist atheism, however reasonable in the concrete situation, has a very serious problem—at the very point of its strength, its concentration upon the theme of man's true reality and emancipation. This is equally true of its positive as of its fundamentally critical emphasis. I would like to pose two basic questions for consideration:

    1. Can we accept the anthropological thesis that man achieves his 'reality' when he 'has himself to thank for his being', and when he is independent of any grace? I cannot accept this thesis. I detect here an abstract and negative concept of freedom. Freedom here means 'independence'. Naturally there is a legitimate element of independence and emancipation in human freedom. But a true freedom is at the same time more: freedom for the other, a fellowship of freedom. Once we have introduced the ideal of *aseitäs* into the understanding of freedom, we have still to define a real concept of man

90

(to say nothing of a true concept of God). An obligation to be thankful and a love which is not deserved love both belong to concrete human freedom. This important part of human freedom, which is clearly expressed in the Christian message of grace and love, brings us into sharp conflict with the positive anthropological teaching of Marx.

2. I do not want to overlook the fact that this one-sidedness in Marx is corrected in other contexts: in his materialistic recognition of the 'need' of the individual man or in his socialistic emphasis on fellowship. As I understand him, even this correction is rendered more difficult by his atheistic attitude, critical to religion. The religious decision for atheism implies that God as the Other, supporting the life of man, is abolished. And this is done in the interest of human emancipation and freedom. Must one accept the thesis that in the interest of emancipation it is necessary to get rid of God?

I am not convinced. No doubt the treatment of God as a 'competitor' to man is found in much bad theology and cheap piety. This concept of God as competing against man appears in Old and New Testament as something abolished, something belonging to an earlier pagan view. It is unbiblical. The God of the Bible is the God of the covenant, of partnership, working for the freedom of man, not his enslavement. From the beginning he is seen as working for the development of man, not for his perpetual adolescence. Think of the Old Testament story of the Exodus and the New Testament account of Jesus Christ! To call upon God is to take an initiative for freedom. The argument for atheism will not hold together. The erasing of God is not a necessary pre-condition of freedom, but a decision about the belief of the unbeliever: an ideological dogma.

This dogma can lead to very considerable

consequences. What does it mean 'to strike out God'? I do not understand it as a purely intellectual operation of ideological cosmetics! Rather is it a potential 'devaluing of all values', and with Marx in a concrete sense, the shifting of the absolute from 'the world of God' to 'the world of men'. In the 'abolition of God' we can by no means be sure that the predicates will disappear with the disavowed subject. They tend to be carried over into a secular context. In the critical operations of dismantling religion the redemption elements of the biblical heritage become secularized. This secularization is a very doubtful operation: the secular questions become 'theologized', 'mythologized' and absolute. Political ideology as the *avant garde* of an absolute future; the field of political action becomes an eschatological battlefield, and finally the political opponent can and does become the apocalyptic power of evil and is understood and treated as such. Legitimate attempts to realize Marxist theory give rise to dangerous consequences—as was carried through in a particularly brutal way by Stalinism.

But I do not wish to be misunderstood. I am not saying that this development, of itself, 'with logical necessity' must arise from the Marxist teaching, and certainly not that it has its origin in the atheistic component of Marxism. I would also maintain that the humanistic concern of Marxism has not been dropped and that there is a real possibility of a correction from within Marxist teaching. It is also my conviction that a critical re-examination of Marxist atheism in its anthropological and dogmatic dimension could play an important role. This would appear to me to be worthwhile. Not that it would make the life of Christians and theologians easier, but rather make all of us much more free for mutual encounter and common social work, as we sharpen and build up our dogmatic criteria.

Is this wishful thinking? If we look at the theory and practice of established Marxism, which despite the disadvantages for life and unity of the citizens of the (east European) socialist states, seems to adhere with astonishing firmness to atheistic dogmas, one may say that it is 'wishful thinking'. Yet, there are also grounds for a quite different attitude and these emerge in the course of dialogue. Some were pointed out in earlier chapters—particularly the first chapter. We shall now turn to the further consideration of one of the most important of these various attitudes: the 'rediscovery' of the biblical heritage on the part of dialogical Marxists.

4. The Dispute over the Biblical Heritage

A Rediscovery

One of the most interesting happenings in the meeting of Christians with Marxists in the 'sixties was the rediscovery of the biblical heritage on the part of some Marxists in the course of the Christian-Marxist dialogue. This is relatively new in the history of Marxist thought.

'Relative' is used because the biblical heritage has played an important role continuously in the form of development of Marxism. This is true especially for Karl Marx himself. That can be understood from his biography. Marx came from a family (both sides) which had lived for generations in the Jewish tradition—intensively and extensively—and the family had embodied this tradition. Among his forbears on his mother's and his father's sides, there was a chain of rabbis and Jewish scholars. Although his father had been converted to the liberal Protestantism of Prussia, he simply could not give up his Jewish culture. Arnold Künzli in his Psycho-biography of Marx rightly describes this culture as 'The pure juice pressed from a heritage which has been lived intensively for centuries, a heritage of Jewish piety and the highest form of Jewish spitituality and learning'.[47]

Naturally the influence of this biblical tradition can be traced in the philosophy of Marx. The fundamental decisions and sensitive attitudes of Marxist theory and practice are quite unthinkable without the biblical background. I mention only a few of the main themes: the serious consideration of history as having meaning and purpose, the high value placed upon labour and its constitutive importance for all that is human, the care for the poor and the oppressed, and the assurance of freedom for the weary and heavy-laden. And the 'Messianic' component: hope for the undoubted coming of redemption and deliverance of human alienation in the post-revolutionary 'kingdom of the free'. Looking at these elements, one can already speak of 'a heavy cargo of biblical energy' in Marxist thought.

The contemporary concern with the Bible is thus not quite new. But without doubt something relatively new has appeared. Most Marxists have not been altogether pleased to see this presence of the biblical heritage in Marxism, but have rather obscured it or even suppressed it. This was particularly true of Lenin's version of Marxism. Yet, even Lenin posed the question quite consciously and systematically about the 'forbears' of Marxism. It was important for him too that Marxist thinking should be established with a legitimate heritage from the best traditions of history. But in the act of determining this best tradition he 'forgot' the biblical component! According to him the 'three sources' of Marxism were German philosophy, English economics and French Socialism. When one looks at the official theory and practice of education in a Lenin-Marxist society, one finds how this has been appropriately worked out. Much comes from the streams of European culture, particularly classical culture, and even more from modern science—but the biblical tradition is left outside standing at the door. If any notice is taken of it at all, it is in atheist propaganda. As a real option, it is, wherever possible, excluded from cultural life (not always successfully).

It was first in the 'sixties that the young Marxists of east and west set up a small protest against this disqualification of the biblical heritage. A new orientation was observed in east and west. In the east, as we have shown in our description earlier of the movement 'From Anathema to Dialogue', a whole group of Marxist philosophers in Czechoslovakia turned their attention to the biblical teaching and its importance for Socialism in the past and present. They set this down in carefully worked studies: the books of Milan Machoveč *(Jesus for Atheism)* and of Vitezslav Gardavský *(God is not quite Dead)* are the best-known among many. In the west, Roger Garaudy in France devoted himself to the question of a possible and meaningful inclusion of biblical themes in Marxism—dealing with the whole range from transcendence to the question of resurrection. Recently there has been the little volume put out by I. Fetscher and M. Machovec *Marxism and the Jesus Affair*. In Switzerland, Konrad Farner, with profound theological understanding has given us works: *Theology of Communism* and *Marxist Salt for Christian Earth—Christian Salt for Marxist Earth*.

In this connection there is one very important thinker whose long life has been concerned with biblical problems as handled by a Marxist and what is more important still, the Marxist interpretation of the Bible: the German Marxist, Ernst Bloch. In this chapter I must discuss what he says in his *Controversy over the Biblical Heritage*.

Bloch's Bible for Revolutionaries

Ernst Bloch is one of the patriarchs of nonconformist Marxist thinkers. In his philosophy the problem of biblical religion was always one of the main themes. It is interesting to note how and to what degree this Marxist has pioneered so many of the themes of modern theology. For example, he was one of the first to take up the theme of the 'Theology of Revolution' which has become so modern among Christians since 1966. As early as 1921 he wrote a book with the title *Thomas Münzer as Theologian of the Revolution*. And that other slogan of modern theology, 'The Theology of Hope', occupied his attention a long time ago. He produced a 3-volume work on *The Principle of Hope* in 1959. So this atheist has broken new ground within the philosophical context of modern theology—he has explored and tested themes which many theologians have later taken up.

Bloch has played this role particularly in his last work. It appeared in Germany in 1968 under the title *Atheism in Christianity* (Suhrkamp Verlag, Frankfurt/M). This book is of very great importance for the atheist reassessment of the Bible in our time. In it Bloch breaks with the traditional Marxist attitude to the Bible (particularly in the 19th century), which has seen the Bible as a religious book and therefore unimportant and uninteresting. He is an apologist for the Bible among Marxists. In the first part of his book he quotes the playright Bertolt Brecht, who when asked what was his favourite reading, replied, 'You'll laugh, but it's the Bible'. That obviously holds for Bloch too. For him the Bible is the most important book in world literature.

It is unique in its formal quality, the richness of its themes and its capacity to deal with all situations. In this, it is incomparable—no other book of world literature could meet all possible actual situations with such facility. But far more important is the content of the Bible. The Bible displays a real breakthrough of true human possibilities, opening up particularly horizons of the future and of hope. Nothing like this can be found in oriental mythology and not very much in Greek philosophy. In the Bible on the other hand lies a unique contribution to human culture, an extraordinarily rich source of stimulus and inspiration. In Bloch's words: 'Thomas Münzer would never have accomplished with Zeus, Jupiter, Marduk, Ptah, etc., what he set in motion with the Exodus from Egypt or the not so gentle Jesus of Nazareth'.[48] The uniqueness of the Bible lies in its revolutionary character. Of course, the Bible is not only a book of revolution. It includes many varied elements and in large areas of it it is certainly also a religious book—'the opium of the people'. So that there are in fact, different Bibles. There is the *biblia pauperum* (the Bible of the poor), the revolutionary book; but so also is there the Bible of the lords and priests; and these two are basically different. Now these different Bibles are interwoven with each other. That is particularly true of the two to which I have referred. Bloch has laid down a hermeneutic principle which can be used by most of us: the later editors have generally tried to cover up or even explain away the original revolutionary message of their forebears. This is how Ezra has been treated in the Old Testament, and the church has done the same with the words of Jesus in the New. If you follow carefully the editorial history of the New Testament, the tendency to remove the revolutionary breakthrough of Jesus and to tone down his words so that he becomes 'gentle and noble', is evident. The humble elements in the Gospel are emphasized.

For the modern philosopher who wishes to interpret the Bible there is much work to be done. He must follow like a detective the latest scholarship, work at the tiresome exegesis and criticism, in order that he may find again the authentic, revolutionary Bible. Bloch undertakes such detective work. In this he cannot build very much upon the theology of the schools. He searches out the most likely scholars and rejects them one after the other, coming at last to the great representatives of the new theology, like Rudolf Bultmann, Karl Barth and Albert Schweitzer. These too he finds inadequate and gives his reasons.

First, he criticizes Bultmann. Bloch examines the programme of de-mythologizing and finds it very confusing. According to Bloch's understanding, Bultmann generalizes where he should not generalize, namely on the problem of mythology itself. And Bultmann declares this problem to be the basic problem of contemporary theology, which it is not. Then the real problem of the biblical message lies in its different types of myth. There is the prophetic myth which courageously attempts to interpret history. And of course there is the religious myth which has to be de-mythologized. Both must be held apart. Now a general concept of myth is affirmed and de-mythologizing in this general sense is declared to be the main task. Then the Bible is necessarily distorted and the basic and progressive dialectical tensions are lost. This too, Bloch blames on Bultmann. What is the outcome of Bultmann's theology? It is simply an understanding of the faith by which the whole community is passionately held together. What remains is a call to existential individuality—but which kind? Bloch does not hesitate to answer his own question— for him it is a bourgeois existence! Bloch does not confine his criticism to Bultmann. He also criticizes Barth and concentrates his attention on the first phase of Barth's theology in the *Commentary on Romans*. He treats him differently. It is quite another matter with Barth, he says. Barth sees the significance of eschatology and that is imortant. But what kind of eschatology? In *Romans* his emphasis is on the 'totally other'. That makes sense, but the radical emphasis on the 'totally other' rules out in any real sense the relevance of this 'totally other' for the situation today. The 'safe stronghold' of transcendence tends to swallow up history.

Bloch's sharpest criticism is reserved for the traditionally liberal interpretation of the Gospel. The classical example is Albert Schweitzer. Schweitzer was one of the first exegetes of the Bible to discover in an ingenious way the importance of the eschatological dimension in the original biblical thinking. Even so, he was also one of the first to declare this eschatology to be irrelevant, at least irrelevant for us. Eschatology has an historic significance, it is the outer cover for the message. In this way he has put it into the background. What remains is a Christ who is the authority for ethical ideas and the motivation for human action. No one should despise that (least of all the example which Schweitzer himself presents), but when it is offered to us as an interpretation of the biblical message then we must reply: 'It is a distorted and', as Bloch himself says, 'dull interpretation of Jesus'.

The leading exponents of Protestant theology do not satisfy Bloch, and so he sets out himself on a fruitful journey into the Bible to find—his own alternative theology. What kind of a journey is this? In a word, it is an atheistic approach to the Bible. The basic principle is 'de-divinize' the Bible. That means: rejection of all elements and themes in which God is presented as 'Lord over all'; resisting all religious 'submission to God above' and all attitudes of passivity and submission. Such attitudes and elements are certainly there in the Bible, but they are not authentic. Bloch understands them as partly priestly interpolations or deliberate falsfications of the original dominantly prophetic message, and partly as symbols or codes, which must be explained. The interpretation of these symbols and codes is now the main task. Bloch takes on this task and in it deals with the main theme of Christian faith. I want to sketch a few examples of such explanations, and first of all the understanding of God.

Bloch takes quite different lines from those taken by the 'death of God' school in trying to understand the problem of God. The God of the meta-physicians (the popular God as well as the God of the philosophers) is certainly dead. But the God of the Bible is the 'I am who I am', or in a better translation of the Hebrew text, 'I will be who I will be'. A coming God, the *deus spes,* 'God Hope'. Not the God of past centuries, but of the future, the God of his Advent. For Bloch, the God of the prophets was not an oriental despot, but the coming 'sea of righteousness'. The God whose kingdom brings peace and freedom for men; whose kingdom is, at the last, man's true home.

He treats Christology in much the same way. Christ can only be understood from the 'orthodox tradition', if we would have a right view of the Christ of the New Testament. The Christology of Modernism fails as christology. The message of the New Testament is not about an ideal man, a religious or moral superman called Jesus of Nazareth. It does not proclaim an ideal of manhood, incorporated in 'gentle Jesus'. The New Testament is concerned with the God-Man. Such is also the theme of orthodox dogma.

Of course this orthodox interpretation of Jesus will be explained in a different way. How does this atheist interpret the Christian dogma? For him, Christ is above all the revelation of the eschatological humanity, the final possibilities of man; radically transcending all former achievements. The Gospel is basically the good news of the limitless possibilities of man.Bloch maintains that this is the heart of the Bible, and not only the New Testament.

He finds something like a preview of the christ-ological message already in the first chapters of the Bible—particularly those passages which do not foretell the coming of Christ! The most important revelation of the true Gospel he finds in unexpected places—even in the mouth of the serpent in Genesis 3, 'You will become as gods'. That is not for Bloch the voice of diabolic temptation. Rightly interpreted this word tells of Christ. Bloch recalls that one of the sects of the early church worshipped Christ under the symbol of the serpent. They had understood Genesis 3 in a deeper sense. They had understood that Christ was in fact the answer to the challenging 'You will become as gods'. Christology is to be understood from that point of view.

That has wide-reaching consequences for the under-standing of our life and of history. *Post Christum natum,* there is for Bloch only one original sin: to refuse to be like God. From that angle the whole Bible must be viewed. That is the norm which alone gives an authoritative meaning, that is the 'canon' of the biblical message.

When you apply that rule to the text it yields unexpected results and certainly unexpected possibilities. Some of the best-known passages in the Bible read very differently when they are interpreted in the light of the words of the serpent! A good example is the Tower of Babel in Genesis 11.

This passage is usually interpreted as a warning against what the Greeks would call *hybris.* Bloch sees such an interpretation as typically priestly. In this passage, there lies no discouraging warning, but originally and in truth, the message of the possibilities of man according to the true Gospel. The tower is an archetype, a sign for the way of mankind out of the Babylonian captivity. In other words, the way of

102

Prometheus, and in this sense an Exodus sign. The way by which later, as Christlike human existence will reveal, all declared impossibilities are transcended.

This human view of destiny is further developed in the main body of the Old Testament. So with Jacob—and he seems to exercise a particular fascination for Marxists, e.g. the Czech philosopher and dramatist V. Gardavský thought of the Jacob story as the key to human history itself—and of course Moses. The Exodus-event with Moses is certainly the central happening of the whole Bible. It gives us the basic message of the Old Testament. There are other witnesses to this view—Job, for example, who is the symbol of the 'promethean Christ' for Bloch. All these figures, the whole 'cloud of witnesses', are witnesses of the true transcendence. In their struggle with (and sometimes against) God they reveal the fundamental possibilities of the promised future of man: 'You shall become as gods'.

Atheistic Christianity—Christian Atheism

Where does Bloch's interpretation finally take us? Turning the pages of his *Atheism in Christianity,* we find the paradox, 'Only an atheist can be a good Christian and only a Christian can be a good atheist'. In this sentence there lies the key to Bloch's ideas. The sentence sounds like a riddle, consciously paradoxical, provoking; but it is easy to see his intention. Both halves of the paradox represent the two fronts on which he is fighting, with his interpretation of the Bible. I must try to explain both halves of Bloch's programme.

'Only an atheist can be a good Christian'. There Bloch has formulated his basic contention. Only the atheist tradition can get the original intention of the Biblical tradition right. This interpretation is certainly very problematic and cannot be accepted in its totality from the standpoint of biblical theology. But as an attempt to bring out one aspect of biblical thinking (and thus to bring it to our attention) it appears to me to be fruitful and original. In an important sense it is no less admissable than the traditional positions— orthodox or liberal. Here is expressed a clear understanding of the dynamic and revolutionary character of biblical faith; without doubt a possibility for understanding the inner core of biblical thinking which must be taken seriously.

An element which one could call 'atheism in Christianity' is certainly there; the tendency of biblical thinking to de-mythologize the world and so to de-divinize; to break up the traditional 'ontocracy', i.e. to overcome the holy mythological interpretation of the universe, in which all things are pre-ordained, pre-determined and sanctified. The Bible questions this view of the universe; it reveals history as the field of meaningful activity. Thus the Bible secularizes and revolutionizes the human experience of the world. Therein, indeed, lies an important aspect of biblical thought which up until now has been very severely neglected by church expositors. In this, Bloch has done a great service; the emphasis on this aspect of the biblical heritage is ecumenically important. In this Bloch belongs to the theology of our day, just as Feuerbach belonged to the theology of the 19th century.

And certainly Bloch also belongs to the atheism of our day. That is shown in the second part of his paradox: 'Only a Christian can be a good atheist'. With this contrary emphasis Bloch fights on his 'second front' against the type of shallow, positivistic atheism. He sees very clearly the danger of a primitive 'free-thinker-ism' and of a vulgar anti-religious propaganda. There is a form of enlightenment which is really a darkening. For Bloch the simple denial of transcendence within the popular, materialistic and positivistic position does not mean progress. It leads to dogmatism or nihilism. As an atheist now Bloch emphasizes this danger of a shallow atheism. And he attempts to do battle on this front inside primitive atheism (including definite types of established Marxism).

A truly liberating atheism is distinguished from the primitive form; it is not the shallow dogmatism of an absolute immanence, but rather a new interpretation of transcendence. 'Christian atheism' in Bloch's meaning of the phrase, is the appearance of that human dimension which is revealed in the Bible and especially in christology: the 'new man' not yet revealed but already coming; the 'not yet' and yet the promise of a future already beginning.

The ultimate goal of all history is the rule of human freedom. It is not yet seen and yet already at hand as man's true home, which overcomes alienation and realized all our divine possibilities. This home is the future, the dimension of the ultimate, to which atheism must remain directed if it is not to degenerate into a vulgar idolatry of immanence. Thus atheism needs the perception of Christianity, Marxism needs it. Otherwise it sinks inevitably into barbarism or nihilism. In this sense, Bloch maintains that only a Christian can be a good atheist.

Without doubt, from both points of view, on both fronts, Bloch's philosophy presents a fruitful possibility. It raises the conversation and the mutual questioning between Marxists and Christians to a new level.

That is Bloch's declared intention. He is particularly concerned to open up and demonstrate this possibility in *Atheism in Christianity*. He is himself aware of how narrow the path is on which he moves. Atheism, like theology, has until now tended to remain unchanged in its irreconcilable and dogmatic ways without much interest in the other side. Despite this, Bloch is deeply convinced that what he calls, 'the unconventional atheistic movement' could in the future begin to read the Bible again. So also, 'unconventional biblical Christians' could become interested again in atheism. Both would profit from reading each other. Atheism would, to its profit, discover new depths of human existence. In this connection Bloch quotes the Russian poet and revolutionary Isaak Babel: 'Banality is the counter-revolution'. It is in the warding off of this danger of counter-revolutionary primitivism that the meeting with Christianity could have great value and importance for the future of atheism.

The same goes for Christianity. If the Christian religion could understand the promethean, active, atheistic and utopian process of humanizing, then it would be able to gain new and progressive insights from its own prophetic tradition. If this encounter is not attempted and realized, then the future of mankind is seriously threatened. Unless this meeting takes place the 'good tower of Babel' will fall into barbarism or nihilism.

Luckily the narrow path and other hopeful possibilities are open: the fruitful encounter between Christians and Atheists in the name of the future of mankind is possible. Bloch concludes with these words:

> 'If on the Christian side, emancipation still means the weary and heavy-laden; if on the Marxist side, the depth of the kingdom of freedom remains the substantial content of revolutionary consciousness and will so remain, then the alliance between revolution and Christianity will not have been ended with the Peasants' war—and next time it will have better success'.[49]

The philosophy of hope hopes also in this respect— for the possibility of significant co-operative work between Christians and Marxists, between theology and philosophy.

We share this hope; it would mean a hopeful and fruitful exchange. But we also share the conviction that a fruitful discussion cannot mean the mixing and blurring of the real differences. This conviction is expressed directly by Bloch in a hopeful commitment to a Christian-Marxist common work and discussion: 'True Marxism takes true Christianity seriously'. And the other way round, we would equally affirm. So, we do not exclude a positive value from Bloch's thinking, but are rather encouraged by it to attempt a critical answer to his atheistic objections, particularly to his atheistic interpretation of the Bible.

A Difficult Path

The basic theses of Bloch's philosophy of hope show that certain definite tendencies of modern thinkers are leading to the conclusion that the gulf between theology and atheistic philosophy need not be destined to be forever unbridgeable. There is a narrow, but visible path out of the dilemma. Shallow atheism and fundamentalist religion may not be reconcilable, but there is a third way. According to Bloch, this lies in the prophetic involvement, by which both philosophy and theology open up the eschatological perspective of hope. This third way is only possible because, according to Bloch, the atheistic interpretation of the Bible has spititual potential, bringing out important emphases which have often been forgotten in the history of hermeneutics, and from which theology and ethics can both learn.

Such interpretation does not concern only details. Much is evident in the new publications of theology which show the influence of Bloch's interpretation. There is W. Zimmerli who in his book *Man and his Hope in the Old Testament* (1968) develops Bloch's understanding of the Old Testament. There is C. H. Ratschow, who has replied to Bloch in his *Atheism in*

107

Christianity? (second edition, 1971). My own little book *Christ or Prometheus?* (1972) could also be mentioned. However, here I want to look at the basic contribution of Bloch to Bible study.

The thesis that the word of the serpent, 'You will become as gods', is the central statement about biblical faith and is to be understood as having this intention, does not at once command acceptance. The whole matter of the biblical message, seen in the light of New Testament christology seems to point in the other direction. Not Man on the way to becoming God, but God on the way to becoming Man, in his incarnation, is the central theme. The theme is developed by the biblical witnesses in many and sometimes richly varied ways: but the 'becoming flesh of the Word', not 'You shall become as gods' is the credal form which is developed in biblical history.

One must not state in this way a false alternative. The 'entry' of God into the history of man is witnessed to, and strengthened, by the Bible. Our life history is taken up into the history of God. but when God receives us he does not disappear from our history. Salvation is promise grounded in transcendence, not the predicate of history. Eschatology is related to history, but history never becomes the eschatological process.

By this I mean the possibilities of the ultimate must not be equated with our ultimate possibilities. The seventh day in which we shall find ourselves, is God's day and not the day of our final victory. Of course this 'Day of the Lord' is our day. The kingdom of God is in fact the Kingdom of our liberation. But this kingdom is the kingdom of God; our final liberation, the last victory over our alienation, happens not because of our efforts and achievements, but in the coming of this kingdom. Therefore the biblical concept of salvation is not bound up with 'Babel', certainly not the 'Tower of Babel', but with the 'New Jerusalem', the coming city of God. The last word belongs not to the 'powerful society' of promethean world conquest—important as this involvement is for the changing of world history— but with the 'community of grace' of the liberated children of God.

I do not criticize Bloch for stating the biblical message in this way—he is not a biblical theologian. His loyalty belongs in the last resort to the philosophy of hope, not the biblical text. The question however is whether his atheistic interpretation of the Bible itself and his philosophy of hope do not rob the Bible of certain meaningful elements; elements which were of considerable significance for the theme which he so passionately advocates: the theme of hope and its anthropological and social implications. I would like to sketch two main lines of criticism and thereby bring both dimensions together. For I believe that by splitting them apart, Bloch has endangered (by his treatment of the Bible) the heart of his own intention—the philosophy of hope.

Can Hope Outlive the Death of God?

According to my understanding, Bloch shatters the ontological foundation of the biblical hope by his atheistic interpretations. I mean the view of the coming kingdom of God as the fulfilment of promise in Christ. The biblical hope is clearly bound up with the vision of transcendent grace, the final redemption from our works and our failures, the victory over the last enemy which is sin and death. Bloch does away with this anchoring of hope in the transcendence of grace, i.e. in God. My question is, 'Can hope outlive "the death of God"?' A few questions, addressed to this root problem of Bloch's philosophy:

What are the categories of a philosophy of hope? That is the fundamental question. What is the 'new'?; what is the 'not yet'? What is the concept of boundary with regard to the future? Are these categories subjective descriptions of human longing, time-bound, anthropomorphic projections onto the objective process of matter and history?

As the title of his book makes clear, *The Principle of Hope,* his central theme is hope, for Bloch not just an anthropological phenomenon, but an ontological principle. It is the key to our understanding of the world, but that is not enough. It is the 'heart of the Thing' itself, matter itself: an ontological principle. Bloch's fundamental thesis and his challenging philosophical programme are put into words in his thoughts on the ontological implications of hope.

This hope is without doubt a human attitude of great weight—*dum spiro, spero* (so long as I breathe, I hope): that is man, *animal sperans*, hoping creature. But is this quality in man anything more than the strong expression of his tragic situation, man who is not only limited, but knows his limitations. This means, man who knows his end is inevitable and tries to fight against that fact. That is undoubtedly an element of high tragedy; but is it more? Religion declares that it most certainly is more. But is it right? Think what Feuerbach says in his criticism—he has analysed the attitude of religious men and called it self-deception. For him this hope is an illusion, an attempt by men to project their dearest wishes onto theological statements and doctrines.

Of course, Bloch knows the criticism of Feuerbach, but he does not accept the ontological consequences and implications of this criticism. He is an atheist, but an atheist of a 'higher order'. The fact must be recognized that there are more things in religion than Feuerbach had ever dreamed of. There is not only the element of illusion, but also the state of consciousness at a deeper ontological level, which traditional materialism has quite frankly overlooked. Religious phenomena are signals of character formations, which in Bloch's theology are the 'new characters' of matter and reality. Hope lights up not only the being of man, but also that of the world. It produces reality on the way. The process of new possibilities requires an open history, an open world. Thus according to Bloch, hope comprises an ontology of hope.

This emphasis on hope carries fruitful and helpful elements in it. For example, the traditional presentation of realism is greatly affected by this point of view. What is realism? That question is often asked today even in political circles. Bloch's contribution is to make clear that realism, in any responsible philosophical sense, cannot be defined simply as something to be recognized for what it is. Realism includes openness towards the new, the 'not yet' character of being. Realism therefore means to struggle to understand the tendency of being (Bloch calls it 'latent tendency of matter-process') and then to deal with it accordingly. In this way the philosophy of hope is revolutionary philosophy. And only those who are revolutionary can be realists. In the thing of realism, the thing itself is dynamic, open, in character utopian.

Even in this connection the ontological problem and the ontological division comes to light. Here Bloch comes up against the most difficult problem of his philosophical study: the difficulty of making clear and demonstrating the identity of human hope as the attitude of hoping creature with the character of hope in being itself.

In relation to this question he formulates the dynamic interpretation of matter. Here he fastens on to Aristotle, for whom matter is possible being, which presses to become real. The category of possibility thus includes both an objective and a subsequent element. The key to this understanding lies in man as historical being. Man will understand as real possibility all that he has become in the course of history and also all that

111

he expects to become in unhindered progress. In this way, man also opens up, in a philosophical sense, the new understanding of matter. In this anthropological context matter can no longer be understood in the mechanical terminology of popular materialism. Rather is it *mater,* the creative mother of a process. With this interpretation, matter is always more than the existing possibilities. Utopian thinking is not unreal, it develops out of the utopian character of matter and is rooted in it.

In this connection some traditional *theological* problems emerge. The human being in the world is characterized by the correspondence between 'the subjective darkness of the fate of his own existence' (the existential moment) and the objective, historical and social given situation, which is open to new possibilities. Now the identity between subject and object is exactly that which one has in the philosophical tradition often designated by the concept of God. Because this identity is the final purpose of the world, it must be stressed that 'God' means not the 'other side' of the world, but ultimately its identity. He is not its identity, but he will be; it is to him that the world goes, he is its Omega of hope, man's hope and the mother process. In this way, Bloch's ontology of hope is complete and it really concerns itself with that which is traditionally the concern of natural theology.

This is where we raise our question. Without doubt, Bloch offers us a wonderful outline. But is this the voice of a necessarily atheistic philosophy? Or do we not rather have here a new breakthrough of a spiritually enriched natural theology; in a real sense perhaps mythology? When one thinks of the fundamental concept of a world process as a self-creating and self-developing move forward, when one describes matter as 'mother' (mother of man and gods), as Bloch does, in reference to a definite mythological tradition, are we not dealing with a new version of ontocracy? Certainly in a dynamic form, but still a version of what was powerfully built into the thought of Greek metaphysics and especially oriental mythology. Being is then understood as a pre-ordained chain of events, holy and ultimately unalterable, in the structures.

My question therefore is: are Bloch's own concepts—the ontological identity of hope-character, of human action with that of being itself—any more than a return to ontocracy?

It seems to me that the spirit of the Bible is quite different and must come into conflict with Bloch's interpretation. The biblical thinking breaks through ontocracy precisely at the point of its commitment to faith in hope, in its vision of the coming God. He comes, not merely as the Omega point, but as the Alpha and the Omega. It is perhaps no accident that Bloch pays little regard to the 'Alpha' of biblical faith. He greatly prizes the Omega, but not the Alpha, the doctrine of creation. There are reasons for this. The biblical view of the creation is one of the Christian presuppositions for the understanding of the world. According to the biblical understanding of creation and in view of the eschatological Alpha and Omega, the world stops short of being an absolute cosmos, the ultimate source of meaning shut up in itself. It is not the Alpha and Omega, but a relative kingdom between Alpha and Omega. It has its 'transcendence', its 'other side', in God. God is not the ultimate identity of what is or what will be; but he is the ultimate judgement and the fundamental hope of what really is.

This point of view breaks through the structure of ontocracy, reduces its fatalistic inclination and shatters the prison of the *status quo.* It opens the revolutionary possibilities of the real Exodus out of human slavery. That is the perspective of hope which does not deceive. He who would have the biblical hope, without this biblical, point of view, seems to me doomed to failure. Here is where the centre of my criticism of Bloch lies. I question whether it is possible to establish the fundamental insights of biblical faith—the dimensions of hope—and at the same time set aside the dimension of the transcendence of grace, as it is understood in the biblical, prophetic tradition.

Worldliness and Grace

This view has consequences for man's social activity. The transcendence of grace as breaking through the ontocratic structures means a radical freedom in the secular realm. The world in which we live is not the ultimate, but the penultimate reality. Human action is secular activity and not the Messianic act, the process of self-redemption. According to the biblical interpretation, man is not burdened with a mission of salvation. He does not have to carry this burden, nor build the new Jerusalem. He is stretched enough in trying to build the human, secular city. He should deploy his whole energy in his own affairs, while the new Jerusalem of our hope sets us free for the secular city. But that New Jerusalem is not the Tower of Babel. We can remain where we are, on the earth. The New Jerusalem comes down, we do not have to climb up to the heavens for it.

This recognition is important for the life of man. If there is anything which endangers the human quality of life, it is the false absolute we ascribe to human activity and our tragic Messianic claims. Now it is my opinion that the 'You shall become as gods' is such a tragic claim because this promise of the serpent places man under a transcendence which is not the transcendence of grace. And so the dilemma is formed, the dilemma of *hybris* or frustration, or a mixture of these two extreme attitudes. The danger which Bloch sees so clearly, of barbarism on the one hand or nihilism on the other, often breaks out precisely at this point where man tries to undertake the task of becoming God.

Here lies the other problem of Bloch's philosophy (or rather mythology) of hope. When Bloch 'deifies' man and the cosmic process, he endangers the worldliness of the world. My view is that we have a strange paradox here: this atheistic interpretation is not secular enough. It leaves the human condition without care for its worldly character. Namely, its real possibility and its real impossibility; its real strengths and its real weaknesses. In a real sense, we have here an example of what in theology we should call a 'Philosophy of Glory'.

A Christian theology can welcome many fresh and stimulating elements in this philosophy. We shall remain thankful that we have this philosophy as a companion in discussion. It is because of this thankfulness that theology will try, in answer, to formulate another, the biblical, view of hope. This is found not in our dreams and in our achievements, both of which Bloch so lovingly describes. The Christian hope stands or falls with the transcendence of grace. It is there that its ontological roots lie. And there also lies its revolutionary challenge, the exodus of the people of God—no blind experiment, but the thankful answer to the promise. In this way we trace a theology of hope and what follows hope; a way without illusions and doubts, without the *hybris* of the Babylonian activists and without the indolence of the pious passivists. Life on the earth is set free from all religious and atheistic mythologies. it is truly secular life which holds itself open for the future of the kingdom of God. Thus we shall try to live our lives as men caught in the tension between radical secularism and radical grace.

That, sketched in a few words, is a provisional answer to Bloch and his meaningful theme 'Atheism in Christianity'. Atheism? yes, but that means the world seen in its radical worldliness. But in the biblical perspective there is seen also the 'infallible hope'. This is hope seen not as the property of the divided possibilities of the world, but as the promise of the kingdom of God. This is the unconditional gift of the loving-kindness of God to the world and to men, rooted in Christ. To witness to this love, to this radical grace as hope, in the confession of faith and in dynamic involvement in the midst of our secular cities: that is my view of the task, and of the justification for a biblical understanding of Atheism in Christianity.

5. Future and Hope in the Christian-Marxist Dialogue

The question of the future is developing into a significant theme of the Christian-Marxist dialogue. A particularly telling example is Bloch's 'dispute over the biblical heritage'. But quite apart from Bloch, there is mutual questioning about the future, both from Marxists and Christians. There are general as well as specific reasons for this. The future has become a threatening problem for us all in the second half of the 20th century. Mankind presses against the limits of his destiny today in a way that is noticeably painful, the limits of his being and his hopes—the limits of growth, of production, of space, and of possible global destruction. In addition, there are the specific problems of a socialistic society. The contrast between the original objectives of Marxist-Socialism and the failures which develop in 'practical Socialism' presents many citizens—particularly the Marxists—with the question of credibility and human competence to achieve future expectations in any real form.

Experience shows that in facing this question there are two blind alleys to be avoided. One is the partly discarded orthodox, ideological line, which for the sake of the grandiose vision projected in its philosophy of history rigorously suppresses the question of concrete personal and present benefits (as typically bourgeois). The other, which is a reaction against this, is the attempt of 'disenchanted' Socialist Pragmatism, for which it appears to be better to forget all about dreams of the future (which turn out quite differently in real life) and to settle for a small, but safer private existence. Involved Marxists and Christians are unable to be satisfied with either of these two options. If we reject these two false alternatives how are we to state and tackle the question of the future and hope? Here we have one of the authentic problem areas of the Christian-Marxist dialogue.

A Common Background

Among the most important things that Christianity and Marxism have in common is that both are consciously orientated towards the future; in both, the theme of 'hope' plays an important role. This relationship goes back to a common heritage in biblical thinking. In the writings of the Old and New Testaments the way is prepared for a truly revolutionary change unique cultural history: pointing to history as a meaningful process. We do not find this in classical antiquity, nor in the ancient orient. In the world of the Bible and earlier, an anti-historical orientation, a mistrust of history, prevailed. Ultimate meaning, salvation, was to be understood as outside time. No hope was to be found in history. The earthly progress was ultimately empty. Indeed, hope itself, in antiquity, is not thought of as a virtue, but the opposite, it is declared a vice, a deception, an illusion.

This is quite different in the Bible, the biblical God

is the God of history. His salvation does not in the first instance lie beyond time, but particularly as salvation in Christ it is in the midst of time, as the goal of history. And above all, his salvation sets history in motion. For this reason, the Bible understands man as an historical man, a pilgrim in time, journeying towards the future. It follows inevitably therefore that hope can no longer be regarded as the attitude of the weak, but must be understood as a cardinal virtue.

This biblical thought, congenial to history, sketches the common background of Christians and Marxists. However, the recognition and value of this thought is not the same in the two families. For the orthodox Marxist the Bible is, as we have already seen, a 'religious' book and therefore a very doubtful source. And yet one can hardly dispute the rich dowry of biblical tradition among the Marxist classics, Karl Marx and Friedrich Engels. Neither is it simply inherited from a particular life style, but a real and continuing stimulus. Above all, apart from other elements already referred to in previous chapters, the element of 'redemption history' directed Marx's theory and practice to the meaningful purpose of history. It is no accident that the positivistic or scientific sceptics of our time attack both movements, Christian and Marxist, for this common attitude, with one breath (e.g. Jacques Monod, in his book *Chance and Necessity*).

This fundamentally common ground in no way means that a quick and easy agreement can be reached. A common heritage does not always guarantee concord, but often the opposite, conflict. This is certainly true of the biblical heritage as understood by Christians and Marxists. The very theme of hope and expectation for the future is a theme of conflict. We shall try to describe this briefly.

To do this, I would like to expound three points, three dimensions of the biblical hope and future expectations:—

119

1. the political dimension
2. the theological dimension, and
3. the personal dimension of hope.

The City of God

I would like to consider a central biblical text: Revelation 21. This is no arbitrary choice. This text played an important role in the 'Prague context' of Christian-Marxist dialogue. Above all, it was important for its connection with certain social initiative which were bound up with it in the thought of the Czech Reformation. Also, the book from which it is taken has received relatively positive comment from the Marxist classical writers.

This chapter, which is one of the most brilliant texts of biblical future expectations, has quite definite outlines which one cannot lightly disregard. At the end of the New Testament, as the final gathering up and validating of history, appears the panorama of the New Jerusalem: a city, which in Greek is *polis* and allows me to speak of a political dimension in the expectation of salvation. The Christian interpretation of hope and the future has this political dimension.

We find similar emphases already in the Old Testament. The Messianic hope of Israel means, not the individual, but the people of God, and from that ultimately, the peoples of the earth. And in the message of Jesus, the coming reality of God is also expressed with a political concept: the kingdom of God. Thus in the view of the Bible, the ultimate reality has community and in this sense political contours.

I want to make this point right at the beginning, because it is often overlooked. The Christian hope and future, the Christian salvation, is often understood as other-worldly, purely spiritual. This is certainly true of the church: when we ask the question of hope or the future with church history in mind, we soon discover

120

a clearly expressed tendency to prefer individualistic and metaphysical answers. Religion is seen as a purely personal affair and the Gospel as comfort for the soul. Until this very day that is the rule widespread among the pious. It is logical enough that those who have rejected the church, atheists and critics of religion, should largely have the same understanding. This is a constant source of Marxist criticism of religion. Religion can be understood in this way as the 'opium of the people'. The church is accused of ignoring social and political reality and blocking all attempts to alter the unjust conditions of earthly life.

This individualistic meaning for the biblical expectation of salvation is, according to my understanding, false, whether it is held by Marxists or Christians. The biblical hope does not betray the earth. The biblical future is not simply concerned with other-worldliness. In its clearest elements it does not tread the way of a disembodied religion. The social message of the time is not overlooked in the message of the prophets and certainly not in the practice of Jesus of Nazareth. This social emphasis is not neglected, but on the contrary, taken up. The promise of the future then has quite concrete lines. It holds for all the afflicted and oppressed, the weary and heavy-laden. And it is on such that our thoughts are fixed when the Bible speaks of salvation and the future.

One has only to think of the 'Beatitudes' of Jesus to understand what the high points of the biblical expectations of the future really are. The poor, the mourners, the meek, those who hunger and thirst after righteousness, the merciful, the peacemakers, those who are reviled and persecuted for righteousness' sake— these are the men spoken of principally in the future, as 'promise', but 'promise' in the Bible does not mean 'comfort' but encouragement and duty to get involved in the future which opens up. This tendency is clear in

121

the expectations of Jesus. It is in this sense that the political dimension of hope must be expressed.

This biblical way of understanding the future has practical consequences.

The Christian hope is politically concerned and orientated. It can never be reduced simply to self-care and religion. The 'New Jerusalem' has something to do with earthly cities. It has something to do with the fate of the poor and the under-privileged in those cities. The Hussites and their predecessors interpreted the Apocalypse in terms of their own projects for practical help, and did not hesitate to link them with the New Jerusalem. Jan Milič from Kromeriz in the 14th century in Prague built a community house for former prostitutes and called it the 'New Jerusalem'. Sentimentality? Hardly, but a sober comment on the free and responsible consequences of Christian hope. The city of God sets the hoping in motion towards the establishing of a just society. In this way, the Christian hope for the future becomes, in the biblical perspective, the practice of hope by a politically-orientated religion.

On this point there is, in the Christian expectation of the future and of salvation, a nearness which the Marxist should note. The political aspect stands uniquely clear,—perhaps as we shall see—unbalanced, in the foreground of the Marxist expectation of the future. It is the strength and the pathos of Marxist thought that it refuses to seek the hope and future of man beyond human society. Only in the 'new city' does the new man achieve his destiny. That is why the Marxist lays such great stress upon the radical changing of the structures and socio-economic relationships of the 'city'. Here lies one of the sharp criticisms made against the Christian, who when he recognizes the 'social dimension' often represents it only in 'charity'. Here the Marxists have grasped, at least in one important point, the consequences of the original biblical view. Here, they are not far from the kingdom of God. Only, in the Marxist sense, this kingdom is the kingdom without God. It is here that we see the parting of the ways between the Christian understanding of Hope and the Future, and Marxist thought.

The Two-Dimensional Man

With that we come to the second dimension of hope and the future—the theological. The city to which John bears witness is not simply a city to your liking. It is the 'New Jerusalem', the city of God. We cannot identify the earthly cities with it without qualification. The hope and future of the Christian cannot therefore be described in terms of any acceptable society—not even eventually with the best of all possible societies. The Christian faith is therefore not in this sense any utopia, or project or expectation of ideal circumstances. But it is hope in the one name, in the name of God.

While I stress this dimension of Christian hope, I must reckon with the fact that for many modern men it sounds alien, clearly not acceptable to Marxists. The connection of hope and expectation of the future with God is unacceptable for most Marxists. This is what they mean by opium of the people. It was expressed quite clearly by the young Karl Marx. I recall once more the important passage: 'A being is only independent when it stands on its own feet and it stands on its own feet only when it is responsible for its own existence. A man who lives by the grace of another considers himself a dependent being'.[50] This holds in general terms for the basis of human emancipation and it holds in particular in relation to God. God is seen as the barrier and the brake on the road to human emancipation.

I take this argument of Marxism seriously. And as a theologian I can only hear it as self-criticism. Karl Marx is not an atheist for reasons of obstinacy or lightly, but as a protest against a church and a theology which in the name of God endangered and hindered the freedom of man. That holds particularly also for the traditional concept of God. How often in theology and church has a concept of God been preached, which was structured on the evident authorities: God as the heavenly superior, who gives authority, in a logical way, to the earthly superiors, 'by the grace of God', as one says. How often this preaching supported and stabilized political conditions.

This theological strategy developed a widespread mentality, as is well known from general church history. This is the way in which the gods of antiquity and of the orient were seen: the undying despots, the keepers of an unchanging order, a kind of cosmic police force! This concept of God has very little to do with the biblical God. The biblical God is no cosmic policeman and no oppressor of men by the exercise of power over them. Quite the opposite. The central events of revelation and salvation in the Old and New Testaments show us a quite different picture of God. Think a moment of the Exodus story in the Old Testament. This decisive salvation event of Israel is at the same time the liberation of slaves to the freedom of the people of God. That is the revelation, that is the purpose of this God: the freeing, yes, rightly understood, the true emancipation of man. And when I think of the New Testament: the way of Jesus in solidarity with the poor and the oppressed, working for their salvation and their well-being, that is the way of God. Clearly no comfort or support for existing conditions, but a challenge in hope. It is this experience, this concern, that the biblically-orientated Christ thinks of when he speaks of the God of hope. Opium of the people? I think not, rather leaven for the future in greater freedom and justice.

What can this understanding of salvation and

expectation for the future in God's name mean for us positively today? What have we to stress here in conversation with Marxists about their expectation for the future? In dialogue with the Marxists, the Roman Catholic theologian, Karl Rahner, has attempted to change the despised and difficult concept of God to one which is real for us. He coins the word 'absolute future'. It may be debated whether such a transcription is helpful. In our discussion however I find such a formula very helpful: the future of man, according to Christian understanding, is not one-dimensional. It has, so to say, two dimensions. It is, of course, in part the relative future—the future of our constructions and plans, our inventions and undertakings, the future of the futurologists, and of the politicians, the technocrats, and also our own private future. This future is largely in our hands. It is also in the hands of our fellow men, known and unknown, and it can quite literally be manipulated and is manipulated.

This future determines our life to a very great extent. But, from the point of view of faith, not yet the whole future of man. In the perspective of Christian hope man has another dimension of the future, what Karl Rahner meant in his concept of 'absolute future': the future before God, the future which is sent by God. Thus man in the light of his future is more than he has in his own hands, more even than he is. In the planned and plannable future he cannot go further: 'It hath not yet appeared what we shall be', so says the apostle (I John 3:2). And he means that we live, not in the straitjacket of a once-and-for-all given situation, but we live in an open perspective, in the horizon of a God-promised and God-given freedom, which is certainly guaranteed.

I believe that just this emphasis, strange though it be, can bring today a free, human situation. More than we know, we live in danger of losing our humanity in that manipulation to which we are prone, handled like objects and manipulated in many different ways: caught in the circle of a hectic, lifeless, everyday life, programmed to the rhythm of production and consumption, performing and consuming. This can take different forms. The temptation is the same—east or west. In the east, of course, there is a greater tendency to total planning; not only political and economic, but also cultural and human life is planned from the centre. But also in the west, in the tendency of a technocratically-orientated society to try to get all men into its grasp by massive economic pressures or seductively by manipulating human needs as labour force or consumer goods. This is the acute danger of our time—the one-dimensional man.

It is here that the message of the future of God, of the absolute future, as the true and inalienable purpose of man, could be helpful. This message prevents, and in a radical manner, the attempt to make man one-dimensional. Human life has more than one dimension. Our existence and our fate, its need and its hope, its present and its future are not completely encompassed by the circle of relativity. Man is, of course, also a relative being. That should not be under-estimated. The absolute future does not destroy the relative future. The God of Jesus Christ is also the God of daily life, as is clearly and wonderfully told in the Gospels. The little sorrows of men, the little hopes, the little happinesses, the little achievements, these can all be meaningful to man and in the highest sense real. But it is not the whole, and must not be made absolute as though it were. Biblically speaking it can be seen as well-being, but not salvation. The salvation of man, his ultimate right, comes from god. And that means that the manipulation of man has its limits.

That holds for my own life, as also and particularly for my dealings with other men. In the light of my own life, I know that I am more than an object, a thing to be manipulated. I am not a slave of impersonal or personal forces. Yes, I am more than the sum of all my performance, certainly more than the sum of all I consume. My right to life is inalienable. This is the true human freedom. And that is freedom's claim on me. I must recognize the same right in my fellow men, respect and claim it for them. When I see man, my fellow man, before God then I know that he is more than the object of my plans and my manipulations. This needs to be put into practice, in relation to my children, in relation to my wife, in relation to my colleagues. It must be shown to be true that I do not have the other in my hands like a one-dimensional object. Only before God, in the perspective of absolute future, do we know man to be truly and certainly a subject, the irreplaceable, unique child of God.

This emphasis of the Christian hope and expectation for the future has its importance for the Marxist interpretation. Marxism erases God and with him the absolute future of man. At the same time, it expects from the historical process, which means from relative future, the ultimate possible solution of human problems, the overcoming of alienation, the healing of the fundamental evil of history. Its future carries a utopian bias. Such an understanding of history will all too easily sacrifice the individual man—in an heroic sense, offered up for the coming generation. This is an attitude of which the serious Marxist is capable and one can but marvel. But there are also problems here, in the temptation to put down other men, in some circumstances even whole generations, in the name of that future.

This temptation has many versions. In a Marxism geared to technology, we come across the tendency to plan men almost totally. In a more ideologically-orientated Marxism, we find the temptation to compel the new men, who may not be ready for the ideological expectations, by acts of force to comply, as in the cultural revolution. From both sides men are sacrificed incidentally as means to an end, albeit a noble and highly commendable end, the just society. This is a risky business and for the personal human life of the actual citizen, a dangerous way.

It was under these circumstances no accident that the question of transcendence, the direct question of God, was opened up anew in the Christian-Marxist dialogue and that it played a notable role even among Marxists! I think of the Swiss, Konrad Farner, the French thinker, Roger Garaudy, and the Czech philosophers whom I have already mentioned in the first chapter, Milan Machoveč, Milan Prucha and Vitězlav Gardavský, with his saying 'God is not quite dead'. Their open attitude did not mean the surrender of atheism, but an attempt to think anew about the humane significance of the Christian expectation for the future.

It was widely recognized that with the concept of God an important condition of human existence was being stated, namely its radical openness: The indication that man and human society took precedence over every ideology, every science, every plan and every achieved condition, including the condition of socialist and communist society. The erasing of God without taking into account this consequence was not enlightenment, but darkening. This was no true emancipation, but rather tutelage; no development, but rather fossilizing of the world of men.

Against the Closing of Existence

With that I come to the third aspect of the biblical understanding of expectations of salvation and the future: the personal dimension of hope. I have chosen this order, the third point, after the section on the political dimension and after the 'absolute future', deliberately. This order is consciously chosen—and polemically meant. Polemically because the traditional way of understanding the Christian expectation of salvation has often been here, and sometimes only here, where our personal fate is concerned. That is for a human point of view understandable and not biblically based.

Biblical hope is not egocentric. It is the kingdom of God and it is first of all theological and political. A church which does not reckon in this way and remains with personal need only, has made a guilty decision. This is particularly true when most of the church members are almost cut off from it and expect just this kind of service when they pay their church tax. A church which fulfils her function still by exercising only her official responsibilities has already been discounted. The private and personal are not the foundations of Christian faith and also not the characteristics of Christian hope. It is for this reason that I have chosen to put the personal aspect last.

Yet, here too we hear the accents of the biblical understanding of hope and expectations of the future. Think once more on the beginning of that selected New Testament text—Revelation 21. In the 'horizontal', the picture of the new city is lit up; in the 'vertical', is heard the voice of God. At the intersection of these two lines a concrete human vision appears: the martyrs, the suffering individuals. It is to them that the deepest human promise is directed: 'He shall wipe away all tears from their eyes—and there shall be no more death' (v. 4).

The two parts of this sentence express two concrete elements of the Christian hope.

1. 'He shall wipe away all tears from their eyes'. This is an astonishing statement. In the political future of god no human tears are trivial. This has nothing to do with the political realists, who often said during the

129

Stalin period, 'When you root out the wood, the splinters fly'. No human need will be swept away from the great table of history; no *tabula rasa* will be made; for God counts every human tear and it will be personally wiped away from the real man. The Christian salvation is salvation with a human face.

With this comment we can see that Christian hope takes the side of our personal life, our human destiny. Before God, it will not be passed over, it will not be written out—in any of its aspects. Our fathers expressed this with the phrase: 'immortality of the soul'. This is a noble thought from ancient Christian spiritual history. In two senses it is liable to misunderstanding: (a) it describes salvation as rescue (or better, flight) from history, (b) it discriminates against the other important part of our human reality, our bodies. Thus, our expectation of salvation and the future loses in this once-honourable phrase, 'the immortality of the soul', two important elements of our corporal-historical, named-personal existence.

Quite other is the biblical hope. It does not strike out history. It is in history that human tears have been shed. And it does not strike out kindness as of little worth. The tears will be wiped from the human face. That means that the ultimate future will not be indifferent to any area of my suffering, my activity, my experience. The hope of antiquity said *non omnis moriar* (I will not completely die); the Christian hope says, almost exuberantly, *omnis non moriar*—my whole life stands in the light of the promise.

2. This concreteness of personal hope is further clarified by the second half of the verse; it is concerned with death: 'And there shall be no more death'. I believe that in this perspective we have the strongest—perhaps it would be better to say most truly human—sense of hope. If death remains undefeated or—as is more often the case—it continues to hang over the future, then the

130

future of man is little more than a respite or the end of the respite, an interim state before the final *nihil,* nothing. Man can live with such a belief, proud, composed—and yes, live with this *nihil,* in the shadow of nihilism.

The biblical hope does not evade death. It identifies it as the last, and positively inescapable enemy of man. And yet, on the basis of the Easter story of Jesus it compels it to capitulate: the last enemy in the world of man is the first conquest in the city of God. 'And there shall be no more death'.

What supports such a statement? Is it simply a pure declaration? I think not. Here reference is made much more to the central experience of the New Testament, the Resurrection of Jesus. It was upon this experience that the church was founded and built; the conviction that in the story of Jesus, his death on the cross was not the final end, but that an unexpected new beginning was found. This experience is understood in the New Testament as an incredible promise. The promise is that our story, in the name of Jesus, with our cross or with our grave, must not be taken as the final end. Here in the face of death the hope of the living God has its right and its validity. This will be said when the promise is for the city of God, and for every citizen suffering under the lordship of death, as for everyone of us personally: 'And there shall be no more death'.

It is this message, certainly difficult to grasp, even in the New Testament beset with many apparent contradictions, which witnesses to more than death in a narrow sense, but against all the powers of death, all that enslaves and shuts up the existence of man. Our existence, open to history is also bound up with the story of Jesus. The message of the Resurrection is identified with the eschatological freedom in the apostolic mission. All 'principalities and powers' are declared powerless and the initiative of hope is shown to be able to rescue the world of man from its inescapable fate. I am convinced that this initiative of hope has remained until this day deep and real for our culture in east and west.

It is astonishing and also a great joy to see that this 'religious' emphasis of the Christian expectation of salvation is being taken up by some present-day Marxists, however critically, in their reflections on the expectation of the future. Marxism has never had any deep concern for the personal questions of death and resurrection. For Marxism, these questions have been secondary, ultimately illusory and superficial. Its way has been the revolutionary way of healing and changing the unjust structures of the contemporary world. This is the way into the future. I understand this involvement of the Marxists, and I think that in this connection Christians have very much to learn from them. It is not only in preaching, but in practice that we must show the world-changing power of hope. Here is a standing need of the church—which has too often been content with words. Salvation today also includes this dimension.

And yet, there is another side. The world-changing activity must not be allowed to make wrestling with questions of the meaning and purpose of personal life superficial. the structural alterations of society do not get rid of the problem of death, rather the contrary. I am reminded once more of experiences in a socialist society. There, the message of the resurrection was no less real, but rather more credible. to take up again the catch-word of 'abdication'. When the church considers this evangelically and carries through its thoughts, then it does not think only in terms of evangelical responsibility, but first of all in terms of service to men. I must say that the churches which truly understood the consequences of abdication were the churches who did not abdicate—not even in a Marxist society!

132

Clearly there was a continuing need among Marxists.

This standing need will in a real sense be discussed here and there within the new Marxism today. I think of my partners in the Christian-Marxist dialogue: again the Czech thinkers like Milan Machoveč and Vitězlav Gardavský, or the Swiss, Konrad Farner. There is an important role to be played especially by Ernst Bloch. This great Marxist authority on the theme of hope does not hide the 'powers of death'. He reckons with the 'messengers of darkness', 'the keeper of death until the last ebbing of life slowly leads to weariness', as still a concern in the best of all societies. But more, he sees in this human, important concern a continuous and never to be ended task of the church, which only the church can do. 'If culture had a plan of campaign directed against the closing of existence, then it is not unthinkable that there should be a commanding general for this campaign'.[51]

Whether the church in her present form—as Bloch suggests—could fulfil this role of general-in-chief for the campaign of hope, has yet to be determined. If this is a challenge to the church, then may I clearly say that I accept it. In our highly developed technological civilization we are threatened with the 'closing of culture'. The campaign against this is due. The light of the biblical perspective—the common heritage of Marxists and Christians—should not be placed under a bushel.

*   *   *   *   *

Notes

1. *Zwischenbilanz* (i.e. Interim Report), quoted in *Der Spiegel* 1974, No. 40, p. 148.
2. *Die Frühschriften,* Marx-Engels; S. Landshut, Stuttgart 1953, p. 216.
3. *op. cit.,* p. 216.
4. *Kleine okonomische Schriften,* Marx-Engels; Dietz-Verlag, Berlin 1955, p. 139.
5. *op. cit.,* p. 139.
6. *op. cit.,* p. 104.
7. *op. cit.,* p. 105.
8. *op. cit.,* p. 98.
9. *op. cit.,* p. 112.
10. *Die Frühschriften,* p. 359.
11. *Kleine ökonomische Schriften,* p. 100.
12. *op. cit.,* p. 98.
12. *op. cit.,* p. 46.
14. *op. cit.,* p. 102.
15. *op. cit.,* p. 104.
16. *op. cit.,* p. 106.
17. *op. cit.,* p. 47.
18. *op. cit.,* p. 108.
19. *op. cit.,* p. 161.
20. *op. cit.,* p. 162.
21. *op. cit.,* p. 162.
22. *op. cit.,* p. 165.
23. *op. cit.,* p. 165.
24. *op. cit.,* p. 140.
25. *op. cit.,* p. 141.

26. *op. cit.*, p. 143f.
27. *op. cit.*, p. 144.
28. *op. cit.*, p. 127.
29. *op. cit.*, p. 132.
30. *op. cit.*, p. 132.
31. *Die Frühschriften*, p. 361.
32. *Kleine ökonomische Schriften*, p. 149.
33. *Sophia und Historie*, Fritz Lieb, Zürich 1962, p. 229.
34. *op. cit.*, p. 230.
35. *Die Frühschriften*, p. 207.
36. *Die Deutsche Ideologie*, Berlin 1953, p. 13.
37. *Die Frühschriften*, p. 207.
38. *op. cit.*, p. 208.
39. *op. cit.*, p. 208.
40. *op. cit.*, p. 208.
41. *op. cit.*, p. 208.
42. *op. cit.*, p. 187.
43. *op. cit.*, p. 204.
44. *op. cit.*, p. 246.
45. *op. cit.*, p. 247f.
46. *op. cit.*, p. 235.
47. *Karl Marx, eine Psychographie*, Arnold Künzli, Wien 1966, p. 35.
48. *Atheismus in Christentum*, Ernst Bloch; Suhrkamp Verlag, Frankfurt/M 1968, p. 22.
49. *op. cit.*, p. 353.
50. *Die Frühschriften*, p. 246.
51. *Naturrecht und menschliche Würde*, Ernst Bloch, p. 311.

Selected Bibliography

Karl Marx : *Economic and Philosophical Manuscripts*
           translated by M. Milligan, Moscow 1957.
—   *Early Writings*
           translated by T. B. Bottomore, London 1963.
—   *The Writings of the Young Karl Marx on Philosophy
           and Society.*
           translated and edited by Lloyd D. Easton and Kurt H.
           Guddat, New York 1967.
—   *Early Texts*
           translated and edited by David McLellan, Oxford 1971,
—   *Critique of Hegel's 'Philosophy of Right'*
           edited with an introduction and notes by Joseph
           O'Malley, Cambridge 1970.

———————————

Thomas J. J. Altizer : *The Gospel of Christian Atheism,* London
                       1967.
B. Delfgaauw : *The Young Marx,* Sheed & Ward, London 1967.
Graeme Duncan : *Marx and Mill : Two Views of Social Conflict
               and Social Harmony,* Cambridge 1973 (This contains
               a very full bibliography).
E. Fromm : *Marx's Concept of Man,* New York 1961.
Roger Garaudy : *From Anathema to Dialogue,* London 1967.
—   *Marxism in the Twentieth Century,* Collins, London
               1970.
—   *The Turning Point of Socialism,* Fontana, London 1970.
—   *The Whole Truth,* Fontana, London 1971.
—   *The Alternative Future,* London 1976.
V. Gardavský : *God is not yet dead,* Penguin 1973.
Helmuth Gollwitzer : *The Christian Faith and Marxist Criticism of
                     Religion,* London 1970.
D. McLellan : *The Young Hegelians and Karl Marx,* Macmillan,
              London 1969.
Milan Machovec : *A Marxist Looks at Jesus,* London 1976.
R. Tucker : *Philosophy and Myth in Karl Marx,* Cambridge 1961.

A Selection from the CJL List

AMIDST REVOLUTION

EMILIO CASTRO

This is an informative book by a leading Latin American who succinctly puts the case for a reappraisal of the Church's role today. Castro's vision of contemporary society and a resumé of the options that are being considered should make Europeans and North Americans search their consciences. For what Latin America is today is in part due to the Church's misunderstanding of its mission and role. How the Second Vatican Council exposes the theological weakness of the Latin American bishops. And how Medellin '68 changed the face of the Catholic Church. Important letters and documents highlighting the changes in the Church's thinking and attitudes are part of this unique book.

Emilio Castro, who is a former President of the Methodist Church in Uruguay and Secretary of the Evangelical Churches Union in Latin America, is a well-known television commentator. Currently he is Director of the Commission on World Mission and Evangelism of the World Council of Churches.

112 pages paperback

£0.90

CHRISTIANS AND CHINA

VICTOR HAYWARD

Written in a popular style 'Christians and China' takes a close look at the analysis of the weakness of the Christian approach. It also looks at the whole question of Christians and Communists in China and how the Church there welcomed the People's Republic. And what of the underground church there today? Hayward looks at China's challenge to the Christian world and raises the question of China's concept of freedom.

This a very readable and informed book
—Life and Work

Victor Hayward was until his recent retirement Research Secretary of the China Study Project at the Selly Oak Colleges in Birmingham, England. A Baptist pastor, he was for 17 years a missionary in China. From 1951-1959 he was General Foreign Secretary of the Baptist Missionary Society. He has edited the series of volumes on 'World Studies of Churches in Mission'.

127 pages paperback

£0.90

PROTESTANTS IN RUSSIA

J. A. HEBLY

Translated by John Pott

'Protestants in Russia' gives:

— a fascinating picture of the development of Protestant groups in Russia up to the present day;
— a clear impression which enters into the feelings, and bears witness to the position, of Protestant Christians under the Soviet administration;
— considerable information on the organization of Christians with respect to communism and the communist government;
— valuable documentation about religious liberty and religious persecution, in this context comes also the existence of the underground church in Russia.

This is one of the best books I have read on the subject of Christians in the Soviet Union
—The Baptist Times

J. A. Hebly was born in the Netherlands in 1923. He studied theology at the University of Utrecht, and was awarded a Doctorate in Theology by that university in 1962.

192 pages paperback

£1.50

EVANGELISM TODAY

Good News or Bone of Contention?

WALTER HOLLENWEGER

In this book Professor Hollenweger takes a sharp look at the biblical understanding of conversion and engages in a process of rethinking evangelism to meet the changing patterns in our society.

Main topics are such controversial issues as the conversion of an evangelist, discovering what the Holy Spirit is doing already in the world. And a critical look at the sermon as a medium of communication; heaven and hell or universalism; the dialogical and situational evangelism of the New Testament.

An excellent and most timely book on the subject has come from the pen of Walter Hollenweger . . . .
—Christian Weekly Newspapers

Walter Hollenweger is a noted Swiss theologian who received his doctorate from the University of Zurich and was for many years an evangelist. A recognized authority on the Pentecostals, he is Professor of Mission at the University of Birmingham, England.

118 pages paperback

£0.90

PENTECOST BETWEEN BLACK AND WHITE

WALTER' HOLLENWEGER

This book offers five case studies on Pentecostalism and politics. It is not only informative and descriptive but is a penetrating analysis of Pentecostalism written in a popular vein. Hollenweger offers an insight into Black Power and Pentecostalism in the United States; an insight into the unique Pentecostalism of Mexico; the catholicity of the Kimbanguists in Zaire; a look at the Holy Spirit and the Virgin Mary in Catholic Pentecostals; and an honest appraisal of the Jesus People. For the first time there is a comprehensive bibliography on the Pentecostals.

To anyone interested in Pentecostalism a book by Walter Hollenweger, ... is a must
—Christian Weekly Newspapers

Walter Hollenweger is Professor of Mission in the University of Birmingham, England. He is one of the world's leading researchers on the subject of the Pentecostal Movement. He has been Secretary for Evangelism in the World Council of Churches.

143 pages paperback

£0.90

HAS THE ECUMENICAL MOVEMENT A FUTURE!

WILLEM A VISSER 'T HOOFT

Few church historians and theologians have equalled this eminent Dutch theologian in putting across difficult and complex issues to the ordinary churchgoer. This is a look from the inside of the Ecumenical Movement by a man who has been at its centre for over 50 years. Visser 't Hooft answers the pertinent questions of today . . . Is the Ecumenical Movement suffering from institutional paralysis? Should the Ecumenical Movement follow the Agenda of the Church or the Agenda of the World? And he takes a penetrating look at the ecumenical witness in the religious world, plus a crisp 'tour de force' of the four periods of modern ecumenical history. This is a revealing assessment at a time of growing international criticism of the World Council of Churches and the Ecumenical Movement. These chapters were the Berkelbach van der Sprenkel lectures in the Netherlands, May 1972.

Since the man . . . has had great influence upon the ecumenical past, his opinion concerning the future of this movement demands respectful attention—Christian Century

97 pages

(cased) £1.60   (paperback) £0.60

INFLATION AND THE COMPROMISED CHURCH

CHARLES ELLIOTT

Written by a professional economist, this is the first attempt to relate the international economic crisis to the Christian faith. In non-technical language the early chapters trace the causes and courses of the international crisis as it has developed in both rich and poor countries. It then seeks to assess who are the real victims of the process. In this situation, does the Christian faith have anything to say? More particularly, are there actions which the individual Christian or the local congregation or the worldwide Church should and could be taking?

Dr Elliott's book is an ironic answer to the many demands that the Church should see inflation as a moral and an economic crisis—The Times

It would be a useful exercise if the British Council of Churches, the General Synod of the Church of England and many other bodies could . . . study and debate this turbulent but expert priest's book
—Church Times

Charles Elliott is Director of the School of Development Studies at the University of East Anglia (England) and Special Adviser to the Parliamentary Select Committee on Overseas Development.

148 pages paperback

£1.20

DATE DUE

GAYLORD